THE LEXICON *of* STUPIDITY

FUN AT PLAY
WHERE IT'S
CREATIVE, SAFE,
WHOLESOME
AND NEUTERING

AD FOR A CHILD-CARE CENTER, MANCHESTER (NEW
HAMPSHIRE) *UNION LEADER*

THE LEXICON
of STUPIDITY

ROSS & KATHRYN PETRAS

WORKMAN PUBLISHING
NEW YORK

ACKNOWLEDGMENTS

This book is as stupid as it is thanks to the help of our smart (and ever-so-patient) editor, Suzie Bolotin, as well as the ever-helpful Megan Nicolay and the ever-creative design team at Workman Publishing.

Library of Congress Cataloging-in-Publication Data

Petras, Ross.
    The lexicon of stupidity / Ross and Kathryn Petras.
        p.cm.
    ISBN-13: 978-0-7611-3791-7
    ISBN-10: 0-7611-3791-2
        1. Quotations, English. 2. Wit and humor.
            3. Stupidity—Miscellanea. I. Petras, Kathryn.
    II. Title.

PN6084.H8P38 2005
082'.02'07—dc22

                                                    2005043650

Workman books are available at special discounts when purchased in bulk for premiums and sales promotions as well as for fund-raising or educational use. Special editions or book excerpts can also be created to specification. For details, contact the Special Sales Director at the address below.

Workman Publishing Company, Inc.
708 Broadway
New York, NY 10003-9555
www.workman.com

Printed in the United States of America
First printing June 2005

10 9 8 7 6 5 4 3 2 1

CONTENTS

INTRODUCTION

Based upon a careful reading of the definition of stupidity, we have noted that the key aspect of stupidity is being stupid or acting stupid or, for that matter, thinking stupid(ly). Indeed, the salient feature of the definition is the repetition of the word *stupid*—which leads us to believe that you (who, may we hastily add, are assuredly

> **stu·pid·i·ty** (stü -'pi-də-tē, styü-) n, pl -ties (1541)
> **1 :** the quality or state of being stupid **2 :** a stupid idea or act

not stupid) have probably by now deduced that the word *stupidity* is based on the word *stupid*. Indeed, you have probably already deduced that this book is about stupidity. (Yes, you are terribly bright.) Perhaps the title tipped you off.

And you are correct. This is a book about stupidity. More specifically, it is a lexicon of stupidity, an alphabetical compendium of the stupidest things ever said, written, printed, or . . . inscribed? Well, perhaps not inscribed. But it is about stupidity. Inadvertent stupidity, to be sure, but stupidity nonetheless.

Other scholars focus on the crème de la crème, turning their eyes to the best and the brightest—the people who have changed the world and the books that have inspired millions. We prefer to focus on a more often overlooked area of human behavior. Our scope is great, ranging from A (Accidents, Traffic) to Z (Zoology, Game Show Contestants' Knowledge of).* And our goal is huge—nothing short of a guided and annotated tour through the stupid things celebrities, athletes, politicians, newscasters, and others have said and the stupid things newspapers, magazines, and Web sites have printed.

So, without further ado, we present the finest of our findings. To quote an appropriate (and intriguing) sign in Taiping Park, Malaysia:

ENJOY.
ENTER WITH YOU OWN RISKS.

ROSS AND KATHRYN PETRAS
New York City

---

*The astute and/or obsessive reader may note that there are no entries for K, M, X, or Y. Why? We don't know.

Accidents, Traffic

Somewhere there's a fascinating statistic about how many traffic accidents occur each day. But you won't read it here. Let's just accept as fact that there are a lot of traffic accidents. And you'd be surprised by how unusual many of them are . . . if you're to believe newspaper reports.

> Her Peugeot 406 estate collided head-on with a fish at the Big Tree Bend, near Inverkeiler.
>
> *ABERDEEN (SCOTLAND) EVENING EXPRESS*

YOUTH HIT BY CAR RIDING BICYCLE

NEWSPAPER HEADLINE

These stories even mention interesting twists on vehicular laws.

> A COMMUNITY POLICEMAN STOPPED HIM FOR NOT RIDING A MOTORCYCLE WHILE WEARING A HELMET, YORK MAGISTRATES HEARD.
>
> YORKSHIRE ENGLAND *EVENING POST*

Celebrities, of course, tend to think they deserve special treatment when they've been in an accident.

"I'M A MOVIE STAR. CAN I TALK TO MY ENTERTAINMENT LAWYER?"

ACTRESS NATASHA LYONNE, WHO STARRED IN *AMERICAN PIE*, TO HER ARRESTING OFFICER IN FLORIDA'S MIAMI-DADE COUNTY (LYONNE WAS ARRESTED ON CHARGES OF DRUNK AND CARELESS DRIVING AND LEAVING THE SCENE OF AN ACCIDENT.)

One final note: We suggest you drive *very* carefully in Fiji . . . because the consequences can be frightening.

According to Colonial War Memorial Hospital staff, the woman was brought in after the accident by witnesses at the scene and was taken in for obliteration.

FIJI *DAILY POST*

Acting, Actors On

If they say so themselves, actors are our new aristocracy. Sometimes these modern-day geniuses descend from their lofty heights to present us, the poor public, with surprising and challenging insights into their chosen medium.

> **In an action film you act in the action. If it's a dramatic film you act in the drama.**
>
> ACTOR JEAN-CLAUDE VAN DAMME, EXPLAINING HIS CRAFT

We also get a fascinating "inside look" at the craft of their trade, at how they deal with, for example, character motivation

> *I loved making* **Rising Sun.** *I got into the psychology of why she liked to get strangled and tied up in plastic bags. It has to do with low self-esteem.*
>
> ACTRESS AND MODEL TATJANA PATITZ

[Starring as Joan of Arc] was incredibly trying on a physical level, but what kept me going was the thought that no matter how difficult it was for me, I knew it had been a lifetime more difficult for Joan.

ACTRESS MILLA JOVOVICH, ON HER ROLE IN *THE MESSENGER: THE STORY OF JOAN OF ARC*

. . . and insights into acting technique.

Charlie Chaplin used his ass better than any other actor. In all of his films his ass is practically the protagonist. For a comic, the ass has incredible importance.

ACTOR ROBERTO BENIGNI

Of course, quality is *always* paramount in the actor's mind.

> I went in and said, "If I see one more gratuitous shot of a woman's body, I'm quitting." I think the show should be emotional story lines, morals, real-life heroes. And that's what we're doing.
>
> ACTOR DAVID HASSELHOFF, STAR OF T&A IIIT *BAYWATCH*

> Beyond its entertainment value, *Baywatch* has enriched and, in many cases, helped save lives. I'm looking forward to the opportunity to continue with a project which has had such significance for so many.
>
> ACTOR DAVID HASSELHOFF

Sometimes actors—those versatile geniuses—become screenwriters. With predictable results.

> **INTERVIEWER:** *You struck gold with* Good Will Hunting. *Are you still writing screenplays?*
>
> **ACTOR BEN AFFLECK:** *I haven't longed to write a screenplay again. I've been writing stuff just personally for me. Just single-word stuff to get me through the day. Sometimes I'll write down just* root *or* energy.
>
> *UNREAL* MAGAZINE

Always, we gain valuable insight into the philosophy of their films and shows.

It answers all the questions, finally, but not really, but kind of.

ACTOR BOB DENVER, DISCUSSING THE TV MOVIE *SURVIVING GILLIGAN'S ISLAND: THE INCREDIBLY TRUE STORY OF THE LONGEST THREE-HOUR TOUR IN HISTORY*

And directors are even *more* insightful.

[I]t just kind of touches on . . . all issues: race, how we treat other cultures, how we treat people, how we treat animals in relation to ourselves. The unanswerable questions: Did we come from evolution? Are we evolving? De-evolving? Darwinism vs. religious beliefs. All of these things, kind of unanswerable things, . . . are symbolized by what *Planet of the Apes* is, and that's the cryptic nature of it.

DIRECTOR TIM BURTON, ON HIS 2001 FILM *PLANET OF THE APES*

Aging

It's easy to understand the concept of aging. We're born in a certain year, and then each year we get one year older. Nice and simple.

Well, not so simple for some. They get stuck on that "each year we get older" part.

> **And here's Moses Kiptanui, the 19-year-old Kenyan, who turned 20 a few weeks ago.**
>
> SPORTSCASTER DAVID COLEMAN

Some people can't grasp the elusive notion that one age isn't the same as another.

> **He's the best 23-year-old catcher I've seen since Campy [Roy Campanella]—and Campy was 25 years old the first time I saw him.**
>
> BASEBALL GREAT CASEY STENGEL

And others seem confounded by age ranges.

> **No, 23 is old. It's almost 25, which is, like, almost mid-twenties.**
>
> SINGER JESSICA SIMPSON

But there's always someone to grab the bull by the horns and make sure age explanation is as clear as can be.

> *Bruce Sutter has been around for a while and he's pretty old. He's 35 years old. That will give you some idea of how old he is.*
>
> SAN FRANCISCO GIANTS
> BROADCASTER RON FAIRLY

Anatomy

Bodies. We all have 'em, and most of us have standard-issue bodies—arms, legs, torso, head, the usual. But certain people seem to have gotten deluxe models.

> ## He lowered one of his three arms to deliver the 30-minute speech.
>
> JOURNALIST TERRY DEYOUNG, IN A NEWSPAPER STORY ABOUT ZIMBABWEAN LEADER ROBERT MUGABÈ

You wouldn't think it, but the elements of anatomy elude many people. They get a little confused about some of the more technical issues, like stomach–skull differences.

> ## MY GUITARS ARE MY UMBILICAL CORD. THEY'RE DIRECTLY WIRED INTO MY HEAD.
>
> METALLICA GUITARIST KIRK HAMMETT

Shoulders can be confusing, too.

And he's got the icepack on his groin there, so it's possibly not the old shoulder injury. . . .

SPORTSCASTER RAY FRENCH

Ian Pearce has limped off with what appears to be a shoulder injury.

SPORTSCASTER TONY COTTEE

Some people are a little shaky on body part identification.

He goes off holding what looks to be a left leg.

SPORTSCASTER PHIL STONE, DESCRIBING INJURED TEXAS A&M PLAYER STEVE KENNY WALKING OFF THE FIELD

Others think body parts may be removable . . .

A tremendous strike, which hit the defender full on the arm . . . and it nearly came off.

SPORTSCASTER BRIAN MOORE

Others think they are definitely removable.

I'M AFRAID THEY'VE LEFT THEIR LEGS AT HOME.

SPORTSCASTER RON ATKINSON

He's pulling off defenders' shoulders and making it difficult for them!

SPORTSCASTER KEVIN KEEGAN

Winfield goes back to the wall. He hits his head on the wall and it rolls off! It's rolling all the way back to second base! This is a terrible thing for the Padres!

SAN DIEGO PADRES ANNOUNCER JERRY COLEMAN, ATTEMPTING TO TELL RADIO LISTENERS ABOUT A LONG FLY BALL HIT BY A MEMBER OF THE OPPOSING TEAM

And sometimes people think body parts are multipurpose!

I know that Gareth Barry has been told by Howard Wilkinson to take a long hard look at these with his left foot.

SPORTSCASTER JOHN MOTSON

Answers, Expert

A lot of newspapers and newsletters have a handy feature: Write in with a question and they'll print the answer for you and other readers.

Yes, in most cases, you will find yourself learning something new, something a lot *different* from what you might have expected.

q: What is the derivation and meaning of the name Erwin?

a: It is English from the Anglo-Saxon and means Tariff Act of 1909.

COLUMBUS (OHIO) *CITIZEN*

Q: *How may slightly soiled playing cards be cleaned?*

A: *They are made by stringing pieces of meat, quarters of onions, and two-inch pieces of bacon on sticks and broiling them over coals.*

THE FLORIDIAN SENIOR MAGAZINE

---

q: What does the thread count printed on the label of bed sheets and pillow cases indicate?

a: The massacre of Fort Mickinac in 1763 by Chief Pontiac of the Ottawas.

COLUMBUS (OHIO) *CITIZEN*

You can even get computer help.
(We use the word *help* loosely.)

q: If I subscribe to a news group, let's say a.b.c., do I automatically get all subgroups, e.g., a.b.c.d, a.b.c.e, etc.?

a: The terminology we should use is: a.b.c is meant for a.b.c is meant for a.b.c only a.b.c* is meant for everything below a.b.c, including a.b.c itself a.b.c* is meant for everything below a.b.c but not a.b.c. a.b.c*, a.b.c.d is meant for a.b.c and below, except a.b.c.d.

NEWSLETTER PUBLISHED BY MIMOS, A COMPANY THAT PROVIDES
INTERNATIONAL INTERNET LINKS

Speaking of using the word *help* loosely . . .

Q: How can you tell the age of a snake?

A: It is extremely difficult to tell the age of a snake unless you know exactly when it was born.

DETROIT NEWS

Even the government has gotten into this "helpful answer" area. So if you have one of those all-too-typical rock-in-my-potato-bag questions, why not ask the Department of Agriculture?

Q: WHAT SHOULD I DO IF I FIND A ROCK IN A BAG OF POTATOES?

A: SIMPLY RETURN THE ROCK TO YOUR GROCER, WHO WILL GIVE YOU THE ROCK'S WEIGHT IN POTATOES.

U.S. DEPARTMENT OF AGRICULTURE BOOKLET
"HOW TO BUY POTATOES"

Answers, Obtuse

Ask a stupid question, get a stupid answer, as the old saying goes. But what about those times when someone asks a straight-forward question and gets a stupid answer?

Take, for instance, this courtroom witness, who definitely seems to have taken her oath to "tell the truth, the whole truth, and nothing but the truth" to heart:

Some of us get a little confused by terms.

> Q: Are you sexually active?
>
> A: No, I just lie there.
>
> COURT TRANSCRIPT

---

q: Did you blow your horn or anything?

a: After the accident?

q: Before the accident.

a: Sure, I played for ten years. I even went to school for it.

COURT TRANSCRIPT

Some people are plagued with very literal minds . . . to the extreme.

REPORTER: Do the Broncos have your number, Christian?

KANSAS CITY CHIEFS' RUNNING BACK CHRISTIAN OKOYE: Do they have my number? I don't know. Do they have a guy with the number 35?

But others are bold enough to answer a question even if they might not really understand it.

REPORTER: Were you apprehensive in the twelfth inning?

BASEBALL GREAT YOGI BERRA: No, but I was scared.

So are we.

Bees

Our friend the honey bee is an important part of our natural world: It pollinates plants and makes delicious honey. So of course bees are a part of our *culture*.

They're featured in books.

And they're featured in films. Hollywood, always quick to spot a trend, has cast numerous bees in several major releases, unfortunately as the *villains*—with predictable, ever classic results.

> I never would have dreamed it would turn out to be the bees! They've always been our friends!
>
> BRAD CRANE (MICHAEL CAINE), *THE SWARM*, 1978

> ARMY OFFICER: You're doing what? Are you mad? You mean you want us to conduct peace negotiations with *bugs*? With *bees*?
>
> SCIENTIST: Either that, or you can consider praying!
>
> *THE BEES*, 1978

Some screenwriters even use elaborate bee imagery.

The peasant is like a wild flower in the forest, and the revolutionary like a bee. Neither can survive or propagate without the other. There is one essential difference between us and the bees, however. In this hive, I will not tolerate drones!

CHE GUEVARA (OMAR SHARIF) TO HIS RAGTAG REBEL ARMY, IN *CHE!*, 1969

Hollywood is, of course, quick to remind us that in *real life,* bees are not monsters or rebels, but true-blue Americans.

The African killer bee portrayed in this film bears absolutely no relationship to the industrious, hard-working American honey bee to which we are indebted for pollinating vital crops that feed our nation.

TITLE CARD AT THE END OF *THE SWARM*, 1978

Unfortunately, in today's urban societies, many people are weak on bee lore.

> DJ: What creature squirts a smelly unpleasant fluid at its enemies?
>
> CONTESTANT: A snake.
>
> DJ: No, I'll give you a clue—it's black and white.
>
> CONTESTANT: A bee.
>
> GAME SHOW ON CAPITAL RADIO (UK)

And the government sometimes is a little *too* strict regarding bees.

> **All bees entering Kentucky shall be accompanied by certificates of health.**
>
> KENTUCKY STATUTE 252.130

Maybe because they've discovered that bees are bad for you.

HIGH CHOLESTEROL LINKED TO EXCESSIVE BEE DIET, TOP DIETITIAN ASSERTS

NEWSPAPER HEADLINE

Beliefs,
Religious

People say you shouldn't discuss religion or politics. One of the biggest problems is that everyone looks at religion a little differently from others. More differently than you might imagine. Take Christianity.

> **HOST ANNE ROBINSON: The four Gospels of the New Testament are attributed to Matthew, Mark, John, and who?**
>
> **CONTESTANT: Joe.**
>
> *THE WEAKEST LINK*

> As a young virgin, the New Testament recounts, Mary was visited by the angel Gabriel who told her that she was to bear Christ's son.
>
> *THE GUARDIAN* (ENGLAND)

Christians believe that Jesus died for our sins and ascended to heaven. Others aren't so sure . . .

HOST ANNE ROBINSON:
Castel Gandolfo is the summer residence of which religious leader?

CONTESTANT: Jesus.

THE WEAKEST LINK

Christianity is divided into many sects, some of which you've probably never thought about.

TELEVISION INTERVIEWER: *I understand that when you were young you were asthmatic.*

PHILIPPINES VICE PRESIDENT JOSEPH "ERAP" ESTRADA: *I beg your pardon! I've always been Catholic.*

Now there's even nude Christianity . . .

One of the things we're trying to get across is, clothes don't promote Christianity.

DAVE PHIPPS, OF DURHAM, NORTH CAROLINA, COMMENTING WHILE ATTENDING A CHRISTIAN NUDIST CONFERENCE, AS QUOTED IN THE *CHICAGO TRIBUNE*

And there's teen-oriented Christianity . . .

THE FIRE OF GOD'S LOVE BURNS OUT THE SIN THE SAME WAY THE HOT STEAM ROUTS THE DIRT OUT OF YOUR PORES.

FROM THE TEEN BIBLE *REVOLVE*, INTENDED TO APPEAL TO TEEN GIRLS

. . . so why not Catholic Judaism?

DJ DURING ON-AIR QUIZ SEGMENT:
What is the nationality of the Pope?

CONTESTANT: *I think I know that one.
Is it Jewish?*

INTERCHANGE ON A PHONE-IN RADIO CONTEST

Most people want their religious leaders to reflect the highest standards of conduct and faith. Others see the ideal a little differently.

> **We'd like to have Baptist ministers and Catholic priests buying and selling drugs, but the real world doesn't operate that way.**
>
> JOHN PASCHALL, ROBERTSON COUNTY (TEXAS) DISTRICT ATTORNEY, COMMENTING ON DRUG ARRESTS AND DEFENDING THE CREDIBILITY OF INFORMER DERRICK MEGRESS

But there is one unifying factor that virtually all religious people can agree on. Religion brings a person peace and comfort in times of great trial and tribulation.

> **[The Kaballah] helps you confront your fears. Like, if a girl borrowed my clothes and never gave them back and I saw her wearing them months later, I would confront her.**
>
> SOCIALITE AND REALITY TV STAR PARIS HILTON, EXPLAINING WHAT STUDYING THE KABALLAH HAS DONE FOR HER

Books

Publishers and writers are worried that the Internet and television are drawing people away from books. How could that be, when there are so many alluring titles* out there, just *demanding* that you pick them up?

- **The Inheritance of Hairy Ear Rims**
- **A Pictorial Book of Tongue Coating**
- **The History and Romance of Elastic Webbing Since the Dawn of Time**
- **A Toddler's Guide to the Rubber Industry**
- **Mucus and Related Topics**
- **Highlights in the History of Concrete**
- **Nasal Maintenance: Nursing Your Nose Through Troubled Times**
- **Big and Very Big Hole Drilling**

The how-to market boasts some particularly intriguing titles.

- *Let's Make Some Undies*
- *Reusing Old Graves*
- *Teach Yourself Alcoholism*
- *Grow Your Own Hair*
- *The Art of Faking Exhibition Poultry*

And then there are those that we're *sure* will wind up on everyone's nightstand.

Be Bold With Bananas

Constipation and Our Civilization

*SOME TITLES NOTED BY *THE BOOKSELLER* MAGAZINE IN ITS ANNUAL ODD TITLE OF THE YEAR CONTEST

Briefings, Pentagon

Pentagon briefings are held to keep the public informed—via the press—about matters of national security. Wait . . . let's rephrase that: They are *theoretically* held to keep the public informed, etc., etc., etc. Why "theoretically"? Let's eavesdrop on one typical Pentagon briefing moment.

REPORTER: *How many NATO strikes have been aborted due to bad weather?*

VICE ADMIRAL SCOTT FRY: *I'm afraid I can't get into that level of detail right off the top of my head.*

REPORTER: *How about an approximation?*

FRY: *I'd prefer not to even approximate it.*

REPORTER: *How about a ballpark figure?*

FRY: *I don't have that information available.*

REPORTER: *How many of [Yugoslavian Premier] Milosevic's surface-to-air missile launchers have been taken out by NATO?*

FRY: *That's a military number I'm not going to talk about.*

REPORTER: *How about a guess?*

FRY: *A large percentage.*

REPORTER: *A large percentage of the missile launchers?*

FRY: *The launchers themselves, no.*

PENTAGON BRIEFING ON THE KOSOVO WAR

What a flood of information! Of course, that's not to say that you can't glean important insights from a Pentagon briefing.

He is either in Afghanistan or some other country or dead.

SECRETARY OF DEFENSE DONALD RUMSFELD, AT A PENTAGON PRESS BRIEFING ABOUT OSAMA BIN LADEN

Government officials really try to clarify things for us.

There are known knowns. There are things we know that we know. There are known unknowns. That is to say, there are things that we know we don't know. But there are also unknown unknowns. There are things we don't know that we don't know.

SECRETARY OF DEFENSE DONALD RUMSFELD, TRYING TO CLARIFY THE WAR ON TERROR DURING A PENTAGON BRIEFING

Needless to say, the president is correct. Whatever it was he said.

SECRETARY OF DEFENSE DONALD RUMSFELD, AT A PENTAGON BRIEFING, AFTER BEING ASKED BY A REPORTER ABOUT COMMENTS PRESIDENT GEORGE W. BUSH HAD MADE

Then there are those times when, in spite of everything, the truth comes out.

That's a good question and let me state the problem more clearly without going too deeply into the answer.

NATIONAL SECURITY ADVISOR BRENT SCOWCROFT, AT A PRESS BRIEFING

Broadcasts, Live

Broadcasting is an active medium—
which means, of course, that we viewers
and listeners can get the news as it is
happening . . . at that very minute!
But what if *nothing* is happening?

> NEWSCASTER PETER SISSONS: How have the
> Chinese reacted to Colin Powell's statement?
>
> REPORTER MATT FREI: Uh, it's the middle of the
> night here and there has been no reaction yet.
>
> EXCHANGE ON THE BBC *TEN O'CLOCK NEWS*, WHEN IT
> WENT LIVE TO HONG KONG TO COVER REACTIONS TO
> THE CAPTURE OF A U.S. SPY PLANE

It's not only news stories that get the "live"
treatment. Reporters also cover human-
interest stories live, with *intriguing* results.

> TELEVISION REPORTER: This November will be your
> 104th birthday. What is your secret for longevity?
>
> ELDERLY MAN: Huh?

Sometimes, for some reason, live news seems a little repetitive.

NEWSCASTER 1: The brief twister or wind gust which hit the area this afternoon also sent a tree right down the middle of a Springfield woman's home. Linda Russell was just feet from where the 40-foot fir crashed through her kitchen, severing her house in the Gateway area. Fortunately no one was injured, although she's not sure where her cat disappeared to. She said the wind lasted only a few seconds.

NEWSCASTER 2: Well, the brief twister or wind gust which hit the area this afternoon also sent a tree right down the middle of a Springfield woman's home. Linda Russell was just feet from where the 40-foot fir crashed through her kitchen, severing her house in the Gateway area. Fortunately no one was injured, although she's not sure where her cat disappeared to—[turns to newscaster 1] We've heard this before, haven't we?

KVAL-TV (EUGENE, OREGON) NIGHTLY NEWS

In answer to that last question, yes, we have, haven't we?

Budgeting

In tough economic times, people know they've got to scrimp. And some make really *big* sacrifices.

Instead [of having] four maids or three maids in the house, you can have two maids.

ABDEL RAHMAN AL-AWADI, KUWAITI MINISTER FOR CABINET AFFAIRS, TELLING HIS COUNTRYMEN HOW TO SAVE MONEY IN POSTWAR KUWAIT

Most of us have stopped using silver every day.

BRITISH PRIME MINISTER MARGARET THATCHER, TALKING ABOUT WAYS OF ECONOMIZING

In other words, they opt for the simple life and do with a little less. They economize on everything from housing . . .

I WANT ONLY TWO HOUSES, RATHER THAN SEVEN. . . .
I FEEL LIKE LETTING GO OF THINGS.

SINGER BARBRA STREISAND

Bureaucracy

People always make jokes about government bureaucracy, but they shouldn't. Bureaucrats are there to help you, the taxpayer.

For example, the government will help you prepare in the event of a fire. It's so clear and simple.

EXIT ACCESS IS THAT PART OF A MEANS OF EGRESS THAT LEADS TO AN ENTRANCE TO AN EXIT.

GOVERNMENT FIRE-PREVENTION PAMPHLET FOR HOMES FOR THE ELDERLY

If you want to change the name of your baby, the government has a special, helpful form for you to fill out.

Said infant is single and has never been married. Said infant has never been convicted of a crime. Said infant's occupation is infant.

APPLICATION FILED BY MOTHER APPLYING FOR A NAME CHANGE FOR HER 2-YEAR-OLD CHILD—FOLLOWING THE LETTER OF THE LAW THAT SAYS THAT A JUDGE MUST BE CONVINCED THAT A PERSON ISN'T CHANGING A NAME TO COVER HIS OR HER TRACKS OR TO DECEIVE THE IRS

Confused about how to figure out leap years? Ask the government!

- Leap year is determined if the 4-digit year can be divided by 4 UNLESS

- The year can be divided by 100, then it is not a Leap Year, UNLESS

- The year can be divided by 400, then it is a Leap Year, UNLESS

- The year can be divided by 4,000, then it is not a Leap Year, UNLESS

- The year is 200 or 600 years after a year that is divisible by 900, then it is a Leap Year

OHIO DEPARTMENT OF ADMINISTRATIVE SERVICES MEMO

And don't worry about your job. The Department of Labor has experts who track employment trends.

The Labor Department said the increase in unemployment last month resulted from workers losing their jobs.

KEYSTONE HEIGHTS, FLORIDA, NEWSPAPER

Of course, bureaucracy has its problems. Periodically, the government tries to streamline procedures . . .

HEALTH DEPARTMENT SAYS DEATH CERTIFICATES ARE TO BE ORDERED ONE WEEK IN ADVANCE OF DEATH.

LANCASTER (OHIO) *EAGLE-GAZETTE*

. . . and then hires more bureaucrats to do all that streamlining.

- Associate Assistant Secretary
- Assistant Assistant Secretary
- Deputy Assistant Assistant Secretary
- Associate Deputy Assistant Secretary
- Chief of Staff to the Associate Assistant Secretary
- Chief of Staff to the Assistant Assistant Secretary
- Principal Deputy to the Deputy Assistant Secretary
- Principal Assistant Deputy Undersecretary
- Associate Principal Deputy Assistant Secretary

JOB TITLES IN THE FEDERAL GOVERNMENT, AS LISTED IN *THE NEW YORK TIMES*

In general, however, government bureaucrats are ready for any eventuality, including an attack on American shores.

If the United States is attacked, file this page in book III of FPM Supplement 990-1, in front of part 771.

Effective upon an attack on the United States and until further notice: a. Part 771 is suspended.

FEDERAL PERSONNEL MANUAL, MANUAL SUPPLEMENT 990-3, CIVIL SERVICE COMMISSION; PART M-771, EMPLOYEE GRIEVANCES AND APPEALS

Celebrities, Bizarro

Maybe it's the air in Hollywood or maybe it's a matter of preselection (in other words, weird people are the ones who become celebrities). Whatever it is, it's clear that a lot of the people we read about in gossip columns are a little . . . yes, different.

They've got the time (and money) to sit back and theorize about things *we never thought about!*

THIS [THE THREADS IN A TWENTY DOLLAR BILL] IS SO THE UNITED STATES GOVERNMENT CAN SCAN YOU. THEY CAN TELL IF YOU'RE CARRYING TOO MUCH CURRENCY. WHEN I SHOWED THIS TO MY HUSBAND, IT REALLY WOWED HIM. WHEN I PULLED OUT THIS LITTLE SPY TRICK, HE KNEW HOW WELL HE'D DONE WITH ME.

ACTRESS PATRICIA ARQUETTE (THEN WIFE OF ACTOR NICOLAS CAGE), DURING AN *US MAGAZINE* INTERVIEW, IN WHICH SHE PULLED OUT A TWENTY-DOLLAR BILL, RIPPED OFF A CORNER, AND POINTED OUT THE THREADS IN THE BILL TO THE REPORTER

They think about deep matters such as life
and death and ask the questions *we might
never have asked* (or answered)!

**Take Ernest Hemingway: Here was a guy who
swallowed, bit, and orally sucked on the long barrel
of a shotgun. What does that tell you? What does it
tell you when a guy—in one of the more exotic
cases I have heard of—hugs a stove, a hot stove, to
death? Horrifying. But what does that tell you?**

ACTOR WILLIAM SHATNER, DISCUSSING SUICIDE

Um . . . what *does* it tell you? Frankly,
we're not sure. But no matter.

See, it's not
easy being
a celebrity.
Some celebri-
ties get a
little peeved
when their
actions are
written up in
the magazines
as if they're
not normal.

**If Michelle Pfeiffer gave Mel
Gibson a vial of blood to wear
around his neck in a movie
you'd think it was terribly
romantic, everyone would cry
and they'd win awards. But in
real life if someone does that
they'd be considered weird.**

ACTOR BILLY BOB THORNTON,
COMMENTING ON HIS THEN MARRIAGE
TO ACTRESS ANGELINA JOLIE—AND
THEIR EXCHANGE OF VIALS OF BLOOD

And, aside from the problems caused by magazines, there are other things that make celebrity life tough. You know, plants . . . or feathers . . . or, of course, antique furniture.

[HOUSEPLANTS] ARE DIRTY. IF I HAVE TO TOUCH ONE, AFTER ALREADY BEING REPULSED BY THE FACT THAT THERE IS A PLANT INDOORS, THEN IT JUST FREAKS ME OUT.

ACTRESS CHRISTINA RICCI

Still, a lot of celebrities are plain ol' folks, just like you and me. Open their refrigerators and you'll see the stuff you'd see anywhere. . . .

I get creeped out and I can't breathe and I can't eat around it. But it's only certain kinds of antique furniture. It mostly . . . has to do with France and England.

ACTOR BILLY BOB THORNTON, ABOUT HIS FURNITURE PHOBIA

"DO NOT EAT"

LABEL ON THE PLACENTA FROM PAMELA ANDERSON'S BABY—
WHICH SHE KEEPS IN THE REFRIGERATOR

So what have we learned? Well, before you grab a snack at Pam's house, make sure you look twice.

Celebrities, Insightful

Nowadays we look to celebrities for everything—including, apparently, cosmological insights.

GAME SHOW HOST: *Which mathematician said, "The most incomprehensible thing about this universe is that it's comprehensible"?*

CONTESTANT: *Mel Gibson.*

2BL 702 RADIO SHOW, AUSTRALIA

All we need to do is to listen to our celebrities and see how they promote a brave new world of, like, learning.

INTERVIEWER: What was the best thing you read all year?

SINGER JUSTIN TIMBERLAKE: You mean like a book?

ROLLING STONE

I'm starting to read to my son. But I couldn't believe how vapid and vacant and empty all the stories were. There's, like, no lessons. . . . There's, like, no books about anything.

SINGER MADONNA, IN AN INTERVIEW ABOUT THE CHILDREN'S BOOK SHE HAD WRITTEN

Christmas

Ah, Christmas . . . Yuletide . . . December 25.

That season of joy, goodwill, peace on earth, and all those wonderful television specials.

> **PERRY COMO'S CHRISTMAS SPECIAL: THE MEMBERS OF A GREEK FAMILY ARE MURDERED SYSTEMATICALLY IN A BIZARRE FASHION.**
>
> *TORONTO SUN* TELEVISION PAGE LISTING

Carolers may come to your door singing, entrancing you with holiday favorites.

> **We now will hear "Deck Your Balls with Halls of Helly" . . . "Deck Your Bells with Balls of Holly" . . . er . . . a Christmas selection.**
>
> BBC RADIO ANNOUNCER

> **"I SAW MURRAY KISSING SANTA CLAUS"**
>
> CHRISTMAS CAROL TITLE LISTED ON A KOWLOON, HONG KONG, SCHOOL HANDOUT

Take a moment to reflect on what this season *really* means.

WHAT WOULD YOU LIKE MOST FOR CHRISTMAS?

FRENCH AMBASSADOR: *Peace throughout the world.*

SOVIET AMBASSADOR: *Freedom for all people enslaved by imperialism.*

BRITISH AMBASSADOR, SIR OLIVER FRANKS: *Well, it's very kind of you to ask. I'd quite like a box of crystallized fruit.*

ASKED OF VARIOUS AMBASSADORS IN 1948 BY A WASHINGTON, D.C., RADIO STATION

Remember, Christmas isn't really as much for us as it is for our children, who are happily awaiting the big day!

CHRISTMAS VACATION ASSIGNMENTS

To aid and guide you on your pathway to learning, the following assignments will help you to activate vehemently your newly acquired aim, "Enthusiasm."

1. A vocabulary test will be given the day you return to school.

2. Oral book reports will be given the first week of school.

MEMO TO NINTH-GRADE STUDENTS BEFORE CHRISTMAS VACATION, QUOTED IN NEIL POSTMAN'S *CRAZY TALK, STUPID TALK*

Communication, Clear

People talk a lot about the breakdown in communication. They worry that people aren't sharing ideas, opinions, and information all that well. We respectfully disagree. The art of communication is alive and well!

Q: DO YOU KNOW IF YOUR DAUGHTER HAS EVER BEEN INVOLVED IN THE VOODOO OR OCCULT?

A: WE BOTH DO.

Q: VOODOO?

A: WE DO.

Q: YOU DO?

A: YES, VOODOO.

ACTUAL TESTIMONY RECORDED IN COURT TRANSCRIPT

The key to good communication is, of course, listening well.

Q: How many trucks do you own?

A: Seventeen.

Q: Seventy?

A: Seventeen.

Q: Seventeen?

A: No, about twelve.

ACTUAL TESTIMONY RECORDED IN COURT TRANSCRIPT

A good translator can work wonders in helping get your point across in a foreign environment.

TRANSLATOR: Yes.

LAWYER: Yes?

TRANSLATOR: Da?

WITNESS: Nyet.

TRANSLATOR: No.

LAWYER: No?

TRANSLATOR: Nyet?

WITNESS: Nyet.

TRANSLATOR: No.

ACTUAL TESTIMONY RECORDED
IN COURT TRANSCRIPT

Good communicators aren't afraid
to ask questions.

LAWYER: Could you briefly
describe the type of
construction equipment
used in your business?

WITNESS: Four tractors.

LAWYER: What kind of tractors are they?

WITNESS: Fords.

LAWYER: You didn't say "four," you just
said "Ford"?

WITNESS: Yes, Ford. That is what you
asked me, what kind of tractors.

LAWYER: Are there four Ford tractors? Is
that what there is?

WITNESS: No, no. You asked me what
kind of tractor it was and I said Ford
tractors.

LAWYER: How many tractors are there?

WITNESS: Four.

ACTUAL TESTIMONY RECORDED IN COURT TRANSCRIPT

And, of course, if they're worried that the person with whom they're speaking doesn't quite get their point, they persevere!

COURT CLERK: Please repeat after me, "I swear by Almighty God . . ."

WITNESS: I swear by Almighty God . . .

CLERK: That the evidence that I give . . .

WITNESS: That's right

CLERK: Repeat it.

WITNESS: Repeat it.

CLERK: No! Repeat what I said.

WITNESS: What you said when?

CLERK: "That the evidence that I give . . ."

WITNESS: That the evidence that I give . . .

CLERK: "Shall be the truth and . . ."

WITNESS: It will, and nothing but the truth!

CLERK: Please. Just repeat after me, "Shall be the truth and . . ."

WITNESS: I'm not a scholar, you know.

CLERK: We can appreciate that. Just repeat after me, "Shall be the truth and . . ."

WITNESS: Shall be the truth and . . .

CLERK: Say, "Nothing . . ."

WITNESS: Okay. [Witness remains silent]

(continued)

CLERK: No! Don't say nothing. Say, "Nothing but the truth . . ."

WITNESS: Yes.

CLERK: Can't you say, "Nothing but the truth"?

WITNESS: Yes.

CLERK: Well? . . . Do so.

WITNESS: You're confusing me.

CLERK: Just say, "Nothing but the truth . . ."

WITNESS: Is that all?

CLERK: Yes.

WITNESS: Okay. I understand.

CLERK: Then say it.

WITNESS: What?

CLERK: "Nothing but the truth . . ."

WITNESS: But I do! That's just it.

CLERK: You must say, "Nothing but the truth."

WITNESS: I will say nothing but the truth!

CLERK: Please, just repeat these four words: "Nothing." "But." "The." "Truth."

WITNESS: What? You mean, like, now?

CLERK: Yes! Now. Please. Just say those four words.

WITNESS: "Nothing. But. The. Truth."

CLERK: Thank you.

WITNESS: I'm just not a scholar, you know.

ACTUAL TESTIMONY RECORDED IN COURT TRANSCRIPT

Congress

How do our elected representatives and senators spend their days? Good question. Actually, according to experts, most of the *real* work is done by the many House and Senate committees.

To: Members of the Committee on Education and the Workforce

Re: Full Committee and Subcommittee Schedule for the Week of May 25–29, 1998.

Monday, May 25, 1998: The Committee is closed in remembrance of Memorial Day.

Tuesday, May 26, 1998: Nothing is scheduled.

Wednesday, May 27,1998: Nothing is scheduled.

Thursday, May 28, 1998: Nothing is scheduled.

Friday, May 29, 1998: Nothing is scheduled.

Senators and representatives often do get together on the chamber floor for exciting debates.

ACTING CHAIRMAN REP. DAN ROSTENKOWSKI (D-ILLINOIS): *Title IX of the recorded bill is now title X.*

REP. WILLIAM L. DICKINSON (R-ALABAMA): *So there is no title IX. There is a title X and we have reopened title VIII, if I am correct.*

ROSTENKOWSKI: *A new title IX was inserted by amendment, so there is now a title IX and a title X.*

DICKINSON: *There is a title VIII, there is a title IX, there is a title X, is that correct?*

ROSTENKOWSKI: *Title X is the last title in the bill.*

DICKINSON: *So an amendment to either title VIII or title IX or title X would be in order at this time?*

ROSTENKOWSKI: *Not title IX. Just title VIII and title X are open to amendment.*

DICKINSON: *Well, I had an amendment that I would like to offer. I thought it was to title IX if there is a title IX.*

ROSTENKOWSKI: *If the gentleman's amendment was drafted to title IX, it will be in order to title X.*

DICKINSON: *Mr. Chairman, I have an amendment at the desk which I would like to offer to title VIII.*

ROSTENKOWSKI: *Title IX of the recorded bill is now title X.*

A FEW MOMENTS OF DISCUSSION ON THE FLOOR OF THE HOUSE OF REPRESENTATIVES IN 1982, AS REPORTED IN *THE WASHINGTON MONTHLY*

Wow! How thrilling to see government in action! Particularly when the legislation being introduced is vital.

One story after another, whether it is taking that Italian classic, *Pinocchio*, or a British classic like *Peter Pan*, he took the past works, added to his own creations, and has given us a timeless legacy where, centuries from now when everybody is forgotten in this House—and I know the President would not mind my saying even Ronald Reagan retreating to a few paragraphs—they will be adding more stereophonic sound quality, more Dolby sound quality and more color enhancement and probably three dimensions to all of these works of Walt Disney. . . . Walt Disney Recognition Day. What a joy!

CONGRESSMAN BOB DORNAN (R-CALIFORNIA), ON OUR IMPORTANT NEW NATIONAL HOLIDAY: WALT DISNEY RECOGNITION DAY

Always one can sense the high intellectual standards of our Congresspeople.

THESE ARE NOT MY FIGURES I'M QUOTING. THEY'RE FROM SOMEONE WHO KNOWS WHAT HE'S TALKING ABOUT.

CONGRESSMAN IN A DEBATE

Mr. Speaker, this bill is a phoney with a capital F.

CONGRESSMAN IN A DEBATE

If you can't visit Washington, may we suggest a visit to your state legislature. You'll be so impressed!

LOUISIANA STATE REP. REGGIE DUPRE (D-MONTEGUT): I CAN'T ACCEPT THIS AMENDMENT, MR. SPEAKER PRO TEMPORE.

LOUISIANA HOUSE SPEAKER PRO TEM PEPPI BRUNEAU (R-NEW ORLEANS): THE AMENDMENT IS BY YOU, MR. DUPRE.

CONVERSATION DURING A SESSION OF THE LOUISIANA STATE LEGISLATURE

Cop Talk

You hear it on TV, you hear it on the streets. You know, that cool-sounding, polysyllabic speech that features, for example, words such as *perpetrator* instead of *criminal*. We call it cop talk. The key seems to be using big words to say very little. Very, *very* little.

REPORTER: Do you have any explanation for the outbreak of weekend robberies?

JOHN B. LAYTON, DISTRICT OF COLUMBIA POLICE CHIEF: The biggest factor is the inclination of certain individuals for acquiring funds by illegal means.

WE HAVE A LOT OF FACTUAL INFORMATION THAT HAS LED TO SPECULATION.

DETECTIVE, AT AN INTERAGENCY MEETING

That clears things up! The problem is, the police officers who have to use those big words very often pick the *wrong* big words.

The muskrat was taken to the Humane Society where it had to be euphemized.

FROM A PRESS RELEASE SENT TO MEDIA BY THE WELLINGTON COUNTY (ONTARIO, CANADA) DETACHMENT OF THE ONTARIO PROVINCIAL POLICE

LAWYER: **AND WAS YOUR RADAR UNIT FUNCTIONING CORRECTLY AT THE TIME YOU HAD THE PLAINTIFF ON RADAR?**

SPEED CHECKED BY RADAR

OFFICER: **YES, IT WAS MALFUNCTIONING CORRECTLY.**

ACTUAL TESTIMONY RECORDED IN COURT TRANSCRIPT

Or they kind of wing it and make big words up as they go.

> **LAWYER:** *Officer, what led you to believe the defendant was under the influence?*
>
> **POLICE OFFICER:** *Because he was argumentary and he couldn't pronunciate his words.*
>
> ACTUAL TESTIMONY RECORDED IN COURT TRANSCRIPT

Other times, they have troubles with some of the smaller words.

WE SHALL OFFER POLICE JOBS TO QUALIFIED WOMEN REGARDLESS OF SEX.

A NEW JERSEY POLICE DEPARTMENT ANNOUNCEMENT

We correctly responded down to the floor above.

POLICE OFFICER

Corrections, Newspaper

You might want to pay more attention to those little newspaper correction boxes that appear on occasion. Some of them are vital, to say the least. Or should we say hair-raising?

CORRECTION

There was an error in the Dear Abby column that was published on Monday. In the fifth paragraph, the second sentence stated that Charlie's hiccups were cured temporarily  through the use of carbon monoxide. It should have read carbon dioxide.

ANCHORAGE (ALASKA) DAILY NEWS

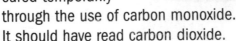

IMPORTANT NOTICE: IF YOU ARE ONE OF THE HUNDREDS OF PARACHUTING ENTHUSIASTS WHO BOUGHT OUR "EASY SKY DIVING" BOOK, PLEASE MAKE THE FOLLOWING CORRECTION: ON PAGE 8, LINE 7, THE WORDS "STATE ZIP CODE" SHOULD HAVE READ "PULL RIP CORD."

A WARRENTON, VIRGINIA, NEWSPAPER

Then again, there are also those that aren't so crucial.

Because of a production error, a picture last Sunday of Prince Charles celebrating the 40th anniversary of Queen Elizabeth's coronation was printed in mirror image. He carried an umbrella in his right hand.

THE NEW YORK TIMES

Counting

It seems that some people need a refresher course in counting. So let's run through a few basic numerical rules.

First, the concept of "two," meaning, well, *two*. Not more than two. Just two.

> **LLEYTON HEWITT—HIS TWO GREATEST STRENGTHS ARE HIS LEGS, HIS SPEED, HIS AGILITY AND HIS COMPETITIVENESS.**
>
> TENNIS COMMENTATOR PAT CASH, COVERING WIMBLEDON

> **The single most important two things we can do . . .**
>
> BRITISH PRIME MINISTER TONY BLAIR

As for "three," the important thing to remember is that three isn't two. *(See above).*

> Chile have three options—they could win or they could lose.
>
> SPORTSCASTER KEVIN KEEGAN

And keep in mind that as numbers increase, they get *larger*. Larger means more. Smaller means less.

> **I WANT TO GAIN 1,500 OR 2,000 YARDS, WHICH- EVER COMES FIRST.**
>
> NEW ORLEANS SAINTS RUNNING BACK GEORGE ROGERS

Got that? Now on to higher mathematics. Like double-digit numbers. The hard-and-fast rule about double-digit numbers is that they consist of *two (see above)* digits.

HOST OF GAME SHOW *WINTUITION*: Name a prime number between 20 and 40.

CONTESTANT: Between 20 and 40?

HOST: Yes.

CONTESTANT: 7.

That's Hendrick's 19th home run. One more and he reaches double figures.

SAN DIEGO PADRES SPORTSCASTER JERRY COLEMAN

Another crucial number rule to remember: You can *add* numbers . . .

We talked five times. I called him twice, and he called me twice.

PHILADELPHIA PHILLIES MANAGER LARRY BOWA

. . . or try to.

Former Westminster city council leader Dame Shirley Porter and the four other members make up the "Westminster six."

PUBLIC FINANCE MAGAZINE

Yes, this is all a little complex. But happily for the number-impaired among us, there are *other* people out there who want to make sure it's all perfectly clear.

Mr. Nixon was the thirty-seventh President of the United States. He had been preceded by thirty-six others.

PRESIDENT GERALD FORD

THIS IS LAP 54—AFTER THAT IT'S 55, 56, 57, 58 . . .

AUTO RACING COMMENTATOR MURRAY WALKER

Crime

Read enough crime stories and you get the feeling that anyone—or anything—might be a criminal.

Pope to be Arraigned for Allegedly Burglarizing Clinic

NEWSPAPER HEADLINE

MAN ACCUSED OF SHOOTING NEIGHBOR, DOG HELD FOR TRIAL

HEADLINE, *THE* (HARRISBURG, PENNSYLVANIA) *PATRIOT NEWS*

Mrs. Lea made no mention of the nationality of the kidnappers nor gave details of her husband's discovery, but he was apparently kept in a darkened hut for two days. He had been roughed up and beaten by insects, the police said.

EVENING NEWS (UK)

Sometimes spotting a criminal isn't that difficult, since many criminals are apparently a little out of the ordinary.

A CARPET WAS STOLEN LAST NIGHT FROM RYDE COUNCIL BUILDING. MEASURING ALMOST SIX FEET SQUARE, THE THIEF HAS BAFFLED COUNCIL OFFICERS.

SYDNEY, AUSTRALIA, NEWSPAPER

At other times, it's the weapon that's unusual.

He told police that one of the men menaced him with a wench while the other covered him with a revolver.

OHIO NEWSPAPER

Man Shoots Neighbor with Machete

MIAMI HERALD

Cockroach Slain; Husband Badly Hurt

NEWSPAPER HEADLINE

Or the crime is, well, *different*.

Robert Paschall, Rt. 2, Los Lunas, reported the theft of six inches.

VALENCIA COUNTY (NEW MEXICO) *NEWS* "POLICE BULLETIN"

But if the crime stories worry you, keep in mind that criminals face the most stringent penalties for the most, er, *fowl* of crimes.

The crime bill passed by the Senate would reinstate the Federal death penalty for certain violent crimes: assassinating the president, hijacking an airliner, and murdering a government poultry inspector.

KNIGHT RIDDER NEWS SERVICE DISPATCH

Criminals

It is said that crime doesn't pay. It certainly doesn't for some criminals. Like the ones who pick the worst possible crime scene . . .

MAN IN LINE AT A PHILADELPHIA BANK:
I am a bank robber. Give me the money.

MAN BEHIND MAN IN BANK LINE:
I am a policeman. You are under arrest.

or the criminals who get carried away with writing a polite hold-up note.

THIS IS A BANK ROBBERY OF THE DALLAS FEDERAL RESERVE BANK OF DALLAS, GIVE ME ALL THE MONEY. THANK YOU, RONNIE DARNELL BELL.

NOTE HANDED TO A SECURITY GUARD BY THE WOULD-BE ROBBER (WHO WAS QUICKLY ARRESTED)

Some criminals need to brush up on their basic knowledge of currency . . .

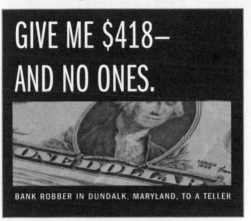

GIVE ME $418— AND NO ONES.

BANK ROBBER IN DUNDALK, MARYLAND, TO A TELLER

while others could use a little work on their anger management.

PROSECUTOR: *Can you identify the man who held up your store?*

WITNESS *[pointing at the defendant]: Yes. That's him.*

DEFENDANT *[leaping up]: I should have blown your f—ing head off . . . , [pause] If I'd been the one that was there.*

ACTUAL TESTIMONY AS RECORDED IN COURT TRANSCRIPT

And they should learn that there is a time and place to be a stickler for accuracy.

CITY MANAGER (to an audience member): Excuse me. No cigarette smoking is allowed. Would you please put out that cigarette?

SMOKER: It's not a cigarette. It's a joint.

INCIDENT AT A MEETING OF THE HARLINGEN, TEXAS, CITY COMMISSION (THE SMOKER WAS ARRESTED FOR POSSESSION OF MARIJUANA.)

Finally, there are those criminals who are just . . . stupid.

BANK ROBBER'S NOTE, HANDED TO TELLER:

Milk, loaf of bread, pick up laundry.

Death

Death is the great mystery. The wise ponder its meaning. Sometimes the not-so-wise throw in a few ideas as well.

FOR MOST PEOPLE, DEATH COMES AT THE END OF THEIR LIVES.

LITERARY REVIEW (ENGLAND)

Some are quite *ambiguous*, shall we say, about the finality and totality of death.

A STRAY BULLET KILLED ONE BYSTANDER SLIGHTLY.

MARYVILLE (MISSOURI) FORUM

Four people were killed, one seriously, and eight more received slight injuries.

JAPAN TIMES

Man Thought Hurt But Slightly Dead

HEADLINE, THE *PROVIDENCE* (RHODE ISLAND) *JOURNAL*

But one thing's for certain: Death isn't fun . . .

The dead also demonstrated a higher level of anxiety than the survived as they found life dull and had more worries. . . . Finally, the dead patients had fewer social contacts and more of them were living alone than the survived.

HONG KONG POLYTECHNIC UNIVERSITY REPORT

. . . although *getting* there can be.

IT IS THOUGHT THAT RAJ MOHAMMED POSELAY WAS BEATEN TO DEATH, POSSIBLY DURING A FAMILY FUN DAY IN THE PARK.

WOLVERHAMPTON (ENGLAND) *EXPRESS & STAR*

Actually, laughing at death is something we shouldn't do. The dead don't like it.

> **We were disturbed by the ridicule because death, especially to the person who has just experienced it, is not funny.**
>
> SPOKESMAN FOR A NATIONAL FUNERAL DIRECTOR'S ASSOCIATION

Nor should we inconvenience others with death. In particular, employees of luxury hotels. The Hilton, for instance.

> *Please tell the public not to kill themselves on hotel property if they want to die. It only confounds us. They can do it in the river for example.*
>
> ASSISTANT PUBLIC RELATIONS MANAGER OF THE JAKARTA HILTON, AFTER A DEATH AT THE HOTEL

Decisiveness

We want leaders to be bold. Strong. Decisive. We want to think that people in charge can make decisions—*decisive* decisions, at that. But try as they might, some leaders don't quite have that decisive thing down pat.

> **RADIO PHONE-IN LISTENER:** Which word best sums up your character?
>
> **BRITISH LIBERAL DEMOCRAT PADDY ASHDOWN:** Uhh . . . perhaps decisive?

I'm not indecisive. Am I indecisive?

JIM SCHEIBEL, MAYOR OF ST. PAUL, MINNESOTA

Sure, politicians do their damnedest to
sound strong and decisive. They even *use*
words like *strong* or *decisive*. It just kind
of . . . peters out at the end, though.

I HAVE OPINIONS OF MY OWN—STRONG OPINIONS—BUT I DON'T ALWAYS AGREE WITH THEM.

PRESIDENT GEORGE H. W. BUSH

Q: *Would you have gone to war against Saddam Hussein if he refused to disarm?*

A: SEN. JOHN KERRY (D-MASSACHUSETTS), THEN CAMPAIGNING FOR THE PRESIDENCY:
You bet we might have.

NEW YORK GOVERNOR MARIO CUOMO, WHEN ASKED ABOUT THE POSSIBILITY OF PRESIDENT CLINTON'S OFFERING HIM A SPOT ON THE SUPREME COURT:

If an offer were made, I would answer the question so swiftly that every one of you in the media, and especially talk-show hosts, would write, "This, surely, is the most decisive man in America."

REPORTER: *Would you accept the offer?*

CUOMO: *I don't know what the answer would be.*

Defenses, Legal

Even when they're guilty, smart criminals know enough not to give the cops anything to work with. That's the essence of a good legal defense. But let's give some time to *bad* legal defense.

> POLICE OFFICER (to purse-snatching suspect in lineup): Put your baseball cap on the other way, with the bill facing front.
>
> SUSPECT: No, I'm gonna put it on backwards. That's the way I had it on when I took the purse.

> DETECTIVE (surveying a line-up): Now each of you repeat the words "Give me all your money or I'll shoot."
>
> SUSPECT IN THE LINE-UP: That's not what I said!

Yes, some criminals would be better off if
they never opened their mouths . . .
Somehow they just, er, lack conviction.

**DEFENSE ATTORNEY: ARE YOU SURE
YOU DID NOT ENTER THE
7-ELEVEN ON FORTIETH AND
NORTHEAST BROADWAY AND
HOLD UP THE CASHIER ON
JUNE 17 OF THIS YEAR?**

DEFENDANT: I'M PRETTY SURE.

ACTUAL TESTIMONY RECORDED IN COURT TRANSCRIPT

Some criminals would be better off if their
defenders never opened their mouths.

For the most part,
he's innocent.

SPOKESMAN FOR RAPPER COOLIO, AFTER HIS
ARREST FOR ALLEGEDLY STEALING $900 AND
ASSAULTING A STORE CLERK IN GERMANY

Sometimes defendants try to get off the hook by explaining that it was all a horrible mistake . . . in a way. They did commit a crime, but they didn't mean to commit that *specific* one.

I MEANT TO KILL MY WIFE, BUT I FORGOT MY GLASSES.

ACCUSED MURDERER OF A PASSERBY

And then there are people who try really hard to be accommodating.

JUDGE: THE CHARGE HERE IS THEFT OF FROZEN CHICKENS. ARE YOU THE DEFENDANT, SIR?

DEFENDANT: NO, SIR. I'M THE GUY WHO STOLE THE CHICKENS.

COURT TRANSCRIPT

On the flip side, there are those who feel that the best defense is a good offense. Or should that be a far-fetched offense?

TESTIMONY OF PLAINTIFF: I am bringing an action for $1,000,000 against a health spa. There, trapped for ninety minutes in the sauna, I changed from a devout Catholic housewife into a raving nymphomaniac.

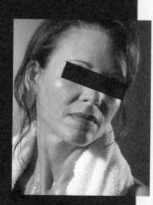

HOUSEWIFE OF 19 YEARS, ACCUSED OF SLEEPING WITH 5,000 POLICEMEN AROUND MEMPHIS, TENNESSEE— CLAIMING THAT THE SAUNA MADE HER DO IT

Diplomacy

The art of diplomacy requires a special set of talents: Tact. Respectfulness. Subtlety.

> **Ireland has food and climate well matched for each other: dull.**
>
> **Pretty small potatoes compared to the other countries in Europe.**
>
> **While Ireland undoubtedly is a great place to visit, living and working here is something else.**
>
> NOTES WRITTEN BY ROBIN BERRINGTON, U.S. CULTURAL AFFAIRS OFFICER, AND MISTAKENLY INCLUDED IN THE U.S. EMBASSY HANDOUT ON IRELAND

A finely honed, rarefied sense of humor is also an asset.

I SEE THE NEW ITALIAN NAVY. ITS BOATS HAVE GLASS BOTTOMS SO THEY CAN SEE THE OLD ITALIAN NAVY.

PETE SECCHIA, WHEN HE WAS GEORGE H. W. BUSH'S NOMINEE FOR U.S. AMBASSADOR TO ITALY (HE WAS APPROVED BY THE SENATE.)

Most diplomats and statesmen have an innate knack for putting people at ease.

DO YOU HAVE BLACKS, TOO?

PRESIDENT GEORGE W. BUSH TO BRAZILIAN PRESIDENT FERNANDO HENRIQUE CARDOSO (NATIONAL SECURITY ADVISOR CONDOLEEZA RICE QUICKLY INFORMED THE AMERICAN PRESIDENT THAT BRAZIL PROBABLY HAS A LARGER BLACK POPULATION THAN THE UNITED STATES HAS.)

YOU KNOW, YOUR NOSE LOOKS JUST LIKE DANNY THOMAS'S.

PRESIDENT RONALD REAGAN TO THE LEBANESE FOREIGN MINISTER, DURING A BRIEFING ON THE REALITIES OF THE MIDDLE EAST CONFLICT

Of course, sometimes things get a little lost in translation.

CHINESE HOST, lifting his glass in a toast to his American guests: Up your bottoms.

AMERICAN DIPLOMAT: Up yours, too.

OVERHEARD AT A COCKTAIL PARTY BOASTING NUMEROUS INTERNATIONAL GUESTS IN SHENYANG, CHINA

But diplomats forge on—determined to make the world a better place, even if their job is a tough one.

I'm the consul for information, but I don't have any information.

CHICAGO ISRAELI CONSUL OFRA BEN YAACOE

Then again, there *are* some hidden perks you might not know about.

ANYTHING CONCERNING THE AMBASSADOR'S SWIMMING POOL MUST BE REFERRED TO AS WATER STORAGE TANK NOT AS SWIMMING POOL.

INTERNAL STATE DEPARTMENT MEMO, U.S. EMBASSY, VIENTIANE, LAOS

Directions, Product

If you were given a packet of peanuts, would you wonder what to do? If so, you can now relax. In the modern world, there are explicit directions on virtually *anything* you buy, including those pesky peanuts.

> **INSTRUCTIONS: OPEN PACKET, EAT NUTS.**
> ON AN AMERICAN AIRLINES PACKET OF NUTS

For nervous drivers, car manuals offer ever-so-helpful hints.

> **To stop the vehicle, release the accelerator pedal and apply the brakes.**
> VOLVO OWNER'S MANUAL

IF YOU CRASH, YOU CAN BE INJURED.

HONDA CRX OWNER'S MANUAL

They even explain highly technical aspects of your car.

The fuel level gauge indicates the quantity of fuel in the tank.

JAGUAR XJ-S OWNER'S MANUAL

The speedometer measures speed.

NISSAN OWNER'S MANUAL

Product information can keep you from making a critical mistake.

Fits one head

SHOWER CAP LABEL

And we thought they fit up to three!

The labels found on food containers are *particularly* helpful. These directions generally revolve around the idea that the food or drink is found *inside* the container, box, or bottle.

FOR BEST RESULTS, REMOVE CAP.

NABISCO EASY CHEESE PRODUCT LABEL

Twist top off with hands. Throw top away.

BOTTLED SOFT-DRINK LABEL

TO BEST ENJOY OUR CEREAL, OPEN BOX.

ON A CEREAL BOX

Education

We all know that a good education is important. So we try to make sure that everyone has access to top-notch, high-quality learning.

But teachers—proud keepers of the educational flame—are worried that students aren't meeting their high standards.

Why is he not learning or leaning so but so little, with my help. How comes his past teachers have been passing him from grade to grade without he advancing or progressing academicly. I will like to know what is causing the mental blockage.

STUDENT EVALUATION WRITTEN BY BROOKLYN, NEW YORK, ELEMENTARY SCHOOL TEACHER

And so we ask:

Are Young Americans Be Getting Stupider?

HEADLINE, CORVALLIS (OREGON) *GAZETTE-TIMES*

Are they be? It sure seem that way.

Illiteracy Is Still a Poblem Among Mississippi Adults

HEADLINE, HENDERSONVILLE (MISSISSIPPI) *TIMES-NEWS*

Maybe the "poblem" lies not in our stars, but in our local institutions and leaders . . .

Commissioner Davis to Head "Assault on Literacy Month"

HEADLINE, PAHOKEE (FLORIDA) *SUN*

EVERYTHING YOU WANTED TO KNOW ABOUT HIGH SCHOOL BUT WAS AFRAID TO ASK

FLYER SENT TO PARENTS BY A LONG ISLAND, NEW YORK, SCHOOL

Or maybe it goes higher than that.

THEN YOU WAKE UP AT THE HIGH SCHOOL LEVEL AND FIND OUT THAT THE ILLITERACY LEVEL OF OUR CHILDREN ARE APPALLING.

PRESIDENT GEORGE W. BUSH

It sure are, aren't it?

Egos

Celebrities are famous for having big egos. Massive, annoyingly overblown egos. But if you ask them about it, they completely disagree.

> I'm sincere. I'm really curious. I care what people think. I listen to answers and leave my ego at the door. I don't use the word 'I.'
>
> TALK SHOW HOST LARRY KING TO A *PSYCHOLOGY TODAY* INTERVIEWER, EXPLAINING WHY HE IS GOOD AT HIS INTERVIEWING JOB—AND USING SIX "I'S" TO DO SO.

Others are a teeny bit more up-front on the ego issue.

I FEEL LIKE I'M THE BEST, BUT YOU'RE NOT GOING TO GET ME TO SAY THAT.

FOOTBALL PLAYER JERRY RICE

Others are a whole lot more up-front.

> **IT SOUNDS VAIN, BUT I COULD PROBABLY MAKE A DIFFERENCE FOR ALMOST EVERYONE I EVER MET IF I CHOSE TO INVOLVE MYSELF WITH THEM EITHER PROFESSIONALLY OR PERSONALLY.**
>
> ACTOR KEVIN COSTNER

Oookay. Yes, many celebrities don't need to read all those "how to build your self-esteem" books or articles, since they don't have any self-esteem problems.

> Why do people treat me with fun just because I am the biggest, strongest, and most beautiful man in the world?
>
> CALIFORNIA GOVERNOR ARNOLD SCHWARZENEGGER, BACK WHEN HE WAS JUST AN ACTOR

REPORTER: *How would you describe yourself?*

ACTOR JERRY LEWIS: *A multifaceted, talented, wealthy, internationally famous genius.*

They're *secure* in their skills, if they do say so themselves.

Yes, I would defend [Adolf Hitler]. And I would win.

ALAN DERSHOWITZ, HARVARD UNIVERSITY LAW PROFESSOR AND DEFENSE ATTORNEY

And they have a realistic view of themselves— and their effect on others. (Wait. Did we say realistic?)

I'M MAKING A CONSCIOUS DECISION TO TAKE THIS WHOLE JUDAISM THING SERIOUSLY. I THINK THE JEWS NEED ME RIGHT NOW.

NEWSMAN GERALDO RIVERA

To be blunt, people would vote for me. They just would. Maybe because I'm so good-looking. I don't know.

MOGUL DONALD TRUMP, WHEN ASKED IF HE WAS CONSIDERING BECOMING A PRESIDENTIAL CANDIDATE.

People all over the world recognize me as a spiritual leader.

ACTION FILM STAR STEVEN SEAGAL, ON HIS BUDDHIST FAITH

E-mail

E-mail has become part of our everyday lives. Problem is, it can be difficult to master. There are so many complicated techie things to learn!

TECH SUPPORT: How may I help you?

CUSTOMER: I'm writing my first e-mail.

TECH SUPPORT: Okay, what seems to be the problem?

CUSTOMER: Well, I can get the a. But how do I put the circle around it?

CALL TO A COMPUTER TECH-SUPPORT STAFFER

Of course, most of us are e-mail experts now. Certainly the bigwigs in the computer industry are. They know when and how to send the proper e-mail message . . . don't they?

THIS IS A WARNING MESSAGE TO LET YOU KNOW THAT YOUR MAIL IS BOUNCING. IF THIS E-MAIL REACHES YOU, THEN PLEASE DISREGARD THIS MESSAGE.

**THANKS!
SINCERELY,
THE MSN LISTBOT TEAM**

ERROR MESSAGE PERIODICALLY SENT OUT BY MSN'S LISTBOT MAILING-LIST SERVER

One tip: Read your e-mail carefully. If you don't, you might be missing *very* important information.

DATE: Wed, 25 Nov 1998 10:29:56 EST
SENDER: owner-abolition-caucus@igc.org
SUBJECT: un votefff

blaffghhjj

E-MAIL SENT BY PEACE GROUP TO VARIOUS OTHER ORGANIZATIONS

Environment

The environment is important to us all. This logic is inescapable, but some of us feel pressed to state it anyway.

This planet is our home. If we destroy the planet, we've destroyed our home, so it is fundamentally important.

H. ROSS PEROT, BUSINESS MOGUL AND THIRD-PARTY PRESIDENTIAL CANDIDATE

Others have more of a "take-no-prisoners" approach to the environment.

In fact, they don't get all that worked up about so-called "threats to nature."

IT'S UNFAIR THAT THE LAND REMAIN EMPTY AND UNSPOILED.

HUGH STONE, DEVELOPER OF A PROPOSED SUBDIVISION, ON DELAYS IN PERMITS TO BEGIN CONSTRUCTION

The caribou love [the oil pipeline]. They rub against it and they have babies. There are more caribou in Alaska than you can shake a stick at.

PRESIDENT GEORGE H. W. BUSH, ON THE ALASKA PIPELINE

This school of thought thinks these threats are overblown, to say the least.

I happen to be one of those people who thinks the aesthetics of a place are improved by putting a nice transmission line through it.

JO MCELWAIN, CHAIRMAN OF THE MONTANA POWER COMPANY

I've always thought that underpopulated countries in Africa are vastly underpolluted.

LAWRENCE SUMMERS, CHIEF ECONOMIST OF THE WORLD BANK, EXPLAINING WHY WE SHOULD EXPORT TOXIC WASTES TO THIRD WORLD COUNTRIES

It isn't pollution that's harming our environment. It's the impurities in our air and water that are doing it.

VICE PRESIDENT DAN QUAYLE

To these forward thinkers, environmentalists pose the *real* threat. They may even be Commies or Nazis.

The environmentalists' real thrust is not clean air, or clean water, or parks, or wildlife, but the form of government under which America will live. . . . Look what happened to Germany in the 1930s. The dignity of man was subordinated to the powers of Nazism. The dignity of many was subordinated in Russia. . . . Those are the forces that this thing can evolve into.

SECRETARY OF THE INTERIOR JAMES WATT

And if you see a bear, watch out. Many of them are psycho.

[GRIZZLY BEARS] ARE SCHIZOPHRENIC, MANIC-DEPRESSIVE ANIMALS. I DON'T WANT THEM AT ALL IN IDAHO.

REP. HELEN CHENOWETH (R-IDAHO), EXPLAINING WHY SHE OPPOSED A PLAN TO REINTRODUCE GRIZZLY BEARS TO HER STATE

Etiquette

Celebrities meet a lot of people, so they always have to be on their best behavior. This makes them a fascinating source on the finer points of etiquette. They know that humor is a great way of connecting with people, of creating a "warm and fuzzy" feeling. So they often use lighthearted jokes to get everyone relaxed and chuckling.

> **IF THE MEN WANT TO TAKE OFF THEIR JACKETS, FEEL FREE TO. AND IF THE GIRLS WANT TO TAKE OFF THEIR BLOUSES, IT'S ALL RIGHT WITH ME.**
>
> MEDIA MOGUL TED TURNER, ADDRESSING THE NATIONAL PRESS CLUB

What a kidder!

Celebrities also realize it's important to let others know they're *accessible*—so they maintain an openness, a friendliness, and an approachability.

> **SPEAKER OF THE HOUSE SAM RAYBURN (PUTTING ARM AROUND FRANK SINATRA):** *Aren't you going to sing "The Yellow Rose of Texas" for us, Frank?*
>
> **SINGER FRANK SINATRA:** *Take your hands off the suit, creep.*

And in one-on-one conversations, they make every effort to put the other person at ease.

Do you mind if I sit back a little? Because your breath is very bad.

REAL ESTATE MOGUL DONALD TRUMP TO LARRY KING, ON KING'S RADIO SHOW

Of course, most of us don't have servants in our homes. But we can pick up some ideas on how to treat waiters and other service professionals by observing actress Marlo Thomas chatting with her butler, Desmond Atholl, according to his book, *That Girl and Phil.*

Noooooo coooooookies!!! No f——ing cookies! I have guests who want cookies! Just what do you expect me to tell them! You f——ing fool! No cookies because you didn't bother to check! And you're supposed to be in charge! You go and tell my guests that you are so stupid you forgot the cookies!

How dare you serve cold cuts in my house. It's just so low class and common. And white bread and pickles! And my God, meat lasagna!!! F——er, you've done it again.

What about meeting new neighbors? Again, celebrities put their ol' "put 'em at ease" charm to work.

I KNOW WHO YOU ARE. YOU DON'T LIVE HERE, YOU RENT.

ACTRESS SHANNEN DOHERTY TO ACTRESS MOLLY RINGWALD, WHO WAS MOVING INTO THE NEIGHBORHOOD TO DOHERTY'S APPARENT DISPLEASURE

Celebrities also realize that it's important to introduce yourself clearly and succinctly in social situations.

PARTY GUEST:
What's your name?

ACTRESS MIRA SORVINO:
I'm Mira Sorvino, an actress! . . . You have embarrassed yourself more than anyone else could at this party. I've done 15 movies and won an Oscar.

AT AN OPENING PARTY FOR *OPERATION CONDOR*, TO A MAN WHO HAD BEEN CHATTING WITH HER

Events,
Eclectic

Just open your local paper and you can find listings for enough fun happenings to satisfy even the wildest of party animals.

There are "family fun" events that you may never have dreamed of . . .

ON DECEMBER 5TH, COME IN WITH YOUR FRIENDS AND FAMILY AND PAINT YOUR BALLS FOR CHRISTMAS.

LISTING FOR AN ATLANTA, GEORGIA, RESTAURANT EVENT

And there are hands-on learning experiences for those with a strong stomach.

> Marian Baker, Harris Center staff member, will demonstrate and help participants turn window- or road-killed wildlife into museum mounts. . . . Bring a lunch and, if possible, your own road kill, foam or cotton stuffing for the animal, sharp knife and scissors.
>
> PETERBOROUGH (NEW HAMPSHIRE) *TRANSCRIPT*

Some special events seem a little . . . *sloppy.*

> **Skydiver Lands on Beer Vendor at Women's Cole Slaw Wrestling Event**
>
> HEADLINE, PETERSBURG (VIRGINIA) *PROGRESS-INDEX*

Some are a little hard to imagine . . .

Good and old American music will be playing the park all the time. It's a festival that you can find full of "sneakers" feeling there.

DESCRIPTION IN THE ENTERTAINMENT LISTINGS SECTION OF A JAPANESE MAGAZINE, PROMOTING A MUSIC FESTIVAL

And still others just don't seem to be that much fun, for some reason.

IT'S SUMMER TIME!

Bring your children to the Garma Specialty Clinic for Circumcision. (Children and Adults). PAINLESS. BLOODLESS. GERMAN CUT.

AD FROM A NEWSPAPER IN MANILA, PHILIPPINES

Excuses

At one time or another, most people make excuses. The key to a good excuse is, of course, *believability*. For instance, we're sure the IRS believed this one:

> [Paying taxes] was one of the things I was always going to take care of, but sometimes I did not have all the funds available or I did not have all the documents and other materials I needed.
>
> NEW YORK CITY MAYOR DAVID DINKINS, ANSWERING ACCUSATIONS THAT HE FAILED TO PAY HIS TAXES

As you can see, making excuses is a talent. To get yourself out of trouble, it's important to have a sound, reasonable explanation—something anyone could have done.

> I HAD THOUGHT VERY CAREFULLY ABOUT COMMITTING HARA-KIRI [RITUAL SUICIDE] OVER THIS, BUT I OVERSLEPT THIS MORNING.
>
> FORMER JAPANESE LABOR MINISTER TOSHIO YAMAGUCHI, AFTER BEING ARRESTED ON CHARGES OF BREACH OF TRUST IN CONNECTION WITH TWO FAILED FINANCIAL INSTITUTIONS

Admitting ignorance is always a winner.

> ## I don't know every damned thing in that ethics law.
>
> SOUTH CAROLINA STATE SENATOR ROBERT FORD, ACCUSED OF THE UNETHICAL PRACTICE OF USING CAMPAIGN MONEY FOR NONCAMPAIGN PURPOSES—NAMELY, MAILING ADS FOR HIS CAR DEALERSHIP IN CHARLESTON

Whenever possible, *clarify.*

> **REPORTER:** *Why didn't Dick Cheney vote in 14 out of 16 elections in Texas?*
>
> **CHENEY SPOKESMAN DIRK VANDE BEEK:** *He did it whenever he could.*

Or define your terms.

THERE WAS NOT A BREACH OF SECURITY AS SUCH. IT WAS A CASE OF SOMEONE CUTTING A HOLE FROM THE OUTSIDE AND FACILITATING THE ESCAPE OF THREE OF OUR INMATES.

GOVERNOR OF A PRISON IN ENGLAND

And spice up your clarification with an insouciant smidgen of "c'est la vie."

First, it was not a strip bar, it was an erotic club. And, second, what can I say? I'm a night owl.

WASHINGTON, D.C., MAYOR MARION BARRY, AFTER BEING CAUGHT IN A STRIP CLUB

You can even try turning a negative into a positive. Say you're cited for a DUI. And let's say you happen to be the head of a major anti-drinking group. Most of us would panic, but an excusemeister spins.

[BEING ARRESTED ON A DUI] WILL GIVE ME ADDITIONAL INSIGHTS INTO DRINKING AND DRIVING. IT ALLOWS ME TO DO MY JOB EVEN MORE EFFECTIVELY.

SUSAN JOHN, CHAIR OF NEW YORK'S ALCOHOLISM AND DRUG ABUSE COMMITTEE AND SPONSOR OF A "ZERO TOLERANCE" BILL

Flipfloppers

Let's pause now and take a moment to appreciate flipfloppers and wafflers. You know, folks who try to make everyone like them—and say things like . . .

> I guess I would have voted with the majority if it was a close vote. But I agree with the arguments the minority made.
>
> PRESIDENT BILL CLINTON, ON THE 1991 GULF WAR RESOLUTION

Yes. We're talking about politicians.

In an effort to win votes and support, they try to please all the people all the time. They *really* try.

HILLARY CLINTON (THEN RUNNING FOR THE NEW YORK SENATE SEAT): *The fact is, I've always been a Yankee fan.*

HOST KATIE COURIC: *I thought you were a Cubs fan.*

CLINTON: *I am. I am a Cubs fan.*

ILLINOIS-BORN SENATOR HILLARY CLINTON (D-NEW YORK), RESPONDING ON THE *TODAY* SHOW TO CLAIMS THAT HER SUDDEN APPRECIATION FOR THE YANKEES WAS POLITICALLY MOTIVATED

And larger, more pressing issues simply encourage them to stick more closely to their bold "whatever you want" stance.

Thank you for contacting me to express your opposition . . . to the early use of military by the U.S. against Iraq. I share your concerns. On January 11, I voted in favor of a resolution that would have insisted that economic sanctions be given more time to work and against a resolution giving the president the immediate authority to go to war.

SENATOR JOHN KERRY (D-MASSACHUSETTS), JANUARY 22, 1991, IN A LETTER TO A CONSTITUENT

Thank you for contacting me to express your support for the actions of President Bush in response to the Iraqi invasion of Kuwait. From the outset of the invasion, I have strongly and unequivocally supported President Bush's response to the crises and the policy goals he has established with our military deployment in the Persian Gulf.

SENATOR JOHN KERRY, JANUARY 31, 1991, IN A LETTER TO THE SAME CONSTITUENT

Even smaller matters stir their compliant souls.

REPORTER: *Are you a dog person or a cat person?*

REP. JAMES TALENT (R-MISSOURI): *Basically, [I'm] a dog person. I wouldn't want to offend my constituents who are cat people, and I should say that being, I hope, a sensitive person, that I have nothing against cats, and had cats when I was a boy, and if we didn't have two dogs might very well be interested in having a cat now.*

Food Ads

A ds for foods and restaurants make everything seem so tasty, so truly tantalizing!

> **Bay Scallops Freshly Sucked**
>
> A&P SUPERMARKET FLYER, NEW JERSEY

Yum! Talk about mouthwatering. And speaking of water . . . or rather the by-product thereof.

> **Pfeiffer's . . . the beer with the silent P.**
>
> RADIO AD SLOGAN FOR PFEIFFER BREWING COMPANY (WHICH THEY TOOK FROM THEIR SUCCESSFUL PRINT CAMPAIGN, NOT THINKING WHAT IT WOULD SOUND LIKE WHEN SPOKEN ALOUD)

U-PEED-'EM SHRIMP

AD FOR A MONTAUK, LONG ISLAND, RESTAURANT

Some ads make bold product claims.

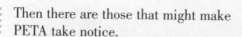

Prize Winning Handmade Sausages:
Once tasted you'll
never want another.

SIGN IN THE OXHEY LANE FARM
SHOP, NEAR GRIMSDYKE, ENGLAND

Then there are those that might make
PETA take notice.

EL PAISANO RESTAURANT

SPECIALIZING IN AUTHENTIC
MEXICAN FOOD *TACOS *
TOSTADAS * BURROS *
ENCHILADAS

AD IN A LOCAL YELLOW PAGES

Kentucky Fried Chicken
Try our new zesty owl.

MARQUEE AD AT KENTUCKY FRIED CHICKEN
(THE B WAS MISSING FROM "BOWL.")

So *that's* what they do when they run out of
chicken.

The Future

Fundamentally, many people agree that the future is where we'll be—in the future. However, some politicians have problems with the exact location of the future.

> I have made good judgments in the past. I have made good judgments in the future.
>
> VICE PRESIDENT DAN QUAYLE

Others are pretty sure where it is.

The future's right in front of us.

SENATOR BOB DOLE (R-KANSAS), IN A CAMPAIGN SPEECH

Some people have strange ideas about the future.

THERE IS CERTAINLY MORE IN THE FUTURE NOW THAN BACK IN 1964.

ROCK MUSICIAN ROGER DALTRY

> ### THAT'S TWICE THAT HAS HAPPENED IN THE RECENT FUTURE
>
> AUTO RACING ANNOUNCER MURRAY WALKER

But we can all agree that . . .

The Future is closer than ever.

ASTROLOGY.COM HOROSCOPE

Geography

A lot of us have problems with geography . . . like, say, knowing where Albania is. But some of us are a bit more challenged than that.

RADIO HOST HOWARD STERN: *What is the capital of New York?*

ACTRESS TORI SPELLING: *New Jersey?*

Yes, some of us get our cities and states kind of mixed up.

I WAS ASKED TO COME TO CHICAGO BECAUSE CHICAGO IS ONE OF OUR 52 STATES.

ACTRESS RAQUEL WELCH, ON HER APPEARANCE AT A PRO-CHOICE RALLY IN CHICAGO

Every city I go to is an opportunity to paint, whether it's Omaha or Hawaii.

SINGER TONY BENNETT

Some of us get our cities and opponents mixed up . . .

REPORTER: *How do you like Los Angeles?*

BOXER PRIMO CARNERA: *I knock him out in two rounds.*

. . . and some of us get our cities and *countries* mixed up.

If I wake up one morning and decide another person can do a better job with this squad, I will tell the wife, "Let's go to Italy." Or Brooklyn. Either one of those countries is fine with me.

PENN STATE FOOTBALL COACH JOE PATERNO, AT A PRESS CONFERENCE

Speaking of countries . . .

YOU MEAN THERE ARE TWO KOREAS?

RICHARD KNEIP, U.S. AMBASSADOR-DESIGNATE TO SINGAPORE, AFTER
BEING ASKED HIS OPINION DURING CONGRESSIONAL HEARINGS ON
THE NORTH KOREA–SOUTH KOREA CONFLICT

It doesn't seem to get easier when countries have been featured on TV news
programs thousands of times.

RADIO HOST HOWARD STERN: *What country
did Saddam Hussein invade during
the Gulf War?*

MODEL AND PENTHOUSE PET SANDI KORN:
Uh . . . what is . . . Jerusalem?

And now, a brief break in defense of Ms.
Korn, who explained:

I am smart, I really am. But Howard asked me about the
war and I was traveling around modeling so much that I
didn't keep track of things like that. I really could have
sworn that we bombed Jerusalem because I have a friend
in Jerusalem and I'm sure he told me Jerusalem was
bombed. But Jerusalem, Iraq—it's all the same anyway.

In the spirit of fairness, however, we must note that perhaps the fault lies not in our stars (or athletes, or ambassador-designates), but in our maps.

The map of Europe, Northern Africa and the Arab nations published in Monday's editions contained the following errors: Libya was labeled as the Ukraine; Bulgaria and Romania were transposed; Bosnia-Herzogovina was identified as Bosnia; Montenegro should have been 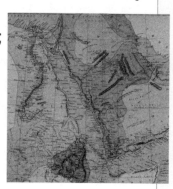 identified as a separate state bordering Serbia; Cyprus and the West Bank were not labeled; Andorra, a country between France and Spain, was not labeled; the Crimean Peninsula appeared twice on the Black Sea; Kuwait was not identified by name—instead, the initials of the Knight-Ridder News Service were in its place.

CORRECTION IN THE NORFOLK (VIRGINIA) *VIRGINIAN-PILOT*

God

God is usually thought of as infinite pure being, beyond what we humble humans can imagine.

GOD'S, LIKE, SO COOL. THINK OF THE COOLEST PERSON IN YOUR LIFE. HE MADE THAT PERSON. AND HE'S COOLER THAN THAT.
ACTRESS JUSTINE BATEMAN

But that doesn't stop Him from being, well, you know, a regular guy . . .

Jesus was—as I like to say—a big moose . . . [not] a little Twinkie. . . . He was a masculine guy.

ROBERT VERNON, ASSISTANT LOS ANGELES POLICE CHIEF, IN AN AUDIOTAPE FROM HIS SERIES "THE TRUE MASCULINE ROLE" RECORDED IN 1977 FOR THE GRACE COMMUNITY CHURCH, SUN VALLEY, CALIFORNIA

Of course, God loves baseball.

I CAN'T PERCEIVE GOD BEING ON THE MOUND IN THE NINTH INNING AND SAYING [A LOSS] IS THE WAY IT SHOULD BE. I PERCEIVE HIM AS BEING AN INDIVIDUAL WHO WOULD BEAT YOU ANY WAY HE CAN AS LONG AS IT'S WITHIN THE RULES.

DICK BALDERSON, SEATTLE MARINERS GENERAL MANAGER

In fact, some Christians see Jesus as really great at sliding into base.

If Christ were a ballplayer, he'd be the best there was. He'd take out the guy at second base, then he'd say, "I love you," pick him up, slap him on the butt, and come back to the dugout.

LOS ANGELES DODGER BRETT BUTLER

Some people say that in addition to running the universe and playing ball, God would find time to be a member of a fraternal organization; maybe pull down a few beers after a game. *Their* fraternal association, of course.

If Jesus Christ was on Earth today, He would be a Shriner.

REV. J. WHITCOMB BROUGHER, D.D.,
OF THE TEMPLE BAPTIST CHURCH,
LOS ANGELES, C. 1925

THERE WAS ONE 100 PERCENT ROTARIAN. HE LIVED 2,000 YEARS AGO. HIS NAME WAS JESUS CHRIST.

BUSINESSMAN HENRY DODGE,
SPEAKING AT THE WILMINGTON,
DELAWARE, ROTARY CLUB

God was the first Kiwanian.

REV. W. F. POWELL, SPEAKING BEFORE THE
KIWANIS CLUB OF COLUMBUS, OHIO

Golf

Golf is a wonderful sport that many people are passionate about. Maybe a little *too* passionate.

Golf is second only to Christianity and is its greatest ally in the development of the highest standard of American manhood and womanhood.

These religious golfers understand the true worth of the game.

Lord, you are more precious than silver. Lord, you are more costly than golf.

Golf and civilization are synonymous, of course.

> **The people don't take baths and they don't speak English. No golf courses. . . . Who needs it?**
>
> QUARTERBACK JIM MCMAHON, ON TRAVELING ABROAD

And the camaraderie among golfers is famous. They all know each other so well!

> **REPORTER:** *What do you think of Tiger Woods?*
>
> **GOLFER SANDY LYLE:** *I don't know. I've never played there.*

But golf can be dangerous. Just ask the NRA . . .

> [A gun is] a recreational tool, like a golf club or a tennis racket. You can kill someone with a golf club, you know.
>
> NRA OFFICIAL MARTEL LOVELACE

Time Out magazine also weighs in.

1:25 Live and Dangerous: European Seniors Tour Golf

TELEVISION LISTING IN *TIME OUT*

Watching golf on TV is not the staid, dull affair many nongolfers claim it is. Just listen to the commentators. They can be very *evocative.*

THE WIND IS RUSHING FROM THE PLAYER'S REAR.

GOLF ANNOUNCER STEVE MELNYK, COVERING A MATCH IN AUGUSTA, GEORGIA

Government

Governments exist to provide order, to promote prosperity, to ensure justice—and to make sure that the public doesn't find out what they're doing. This is, of course, for the public's own good.

> **The meeting was held in secret because it concerns the public so much.**
>
> EDWARD COOPER, MAYOR OF CAINE, WILTSHIRE, ENGLAND, ON A MEETING ABOUT THE POLICE

Sometimes governments say they're going to be more open, with somewhat less than convincing results.

> **The Israeli intelligence community is more open today than it ever has been. This is stated by a top military intelligence officer, Colonel "A," who was speaking to our correspondent.**
>
> ISRAELI DEFENSE FORCES RADIO

They even release documents to Congress and the public.

The [deleted] is a key element of the Worldwide Military Command and Control System (WWMCCS) warning network. . . . [Deleted] currently consists of [deleted] satellite; two [deleted] satellites; an [deleted] for [deleted] from the [deleted] satellite; a [deleted] for [deleted] and the [deleted] satellites; and a [deleted] which provides [deleted] for the [deleted]. . . . Using these data, [deleted] can be inferred.

ARMS-CONTROL IMPACT STATEMENT SUBMITTED TO CONGRESS BY THE PENTAGON

And all in all, they understand that a free citizenry is an informed citizenry.

THE PRESS SAYS THAT THE PUBLIC HAS A RIGHT TO KNOW EVERYTHING. THAT'S A LOAD OF GARBAGE.

CIA SPOKESMAN GEORGE LAUDER

The government has weird ways of defining words, such as *success*.

[The Air Force is pleased with the performance of the C-5A cargo plane, although] having the wings fall off at 8,000 hours is a problem.

MAJOR GENERAL CHARLES F. KUYK JR.

The government certainly doesn't understand the average taxpayer or business.

Optional payment: If you wish to voluntarily pay the maximum assessment . . . send a payment of $250,000.00 to: California Travel and Tourism Commission.

LINE ON THE STATE OF CALIFORNIA TOURISM ASSESSMENT FORM

Bribes and kickbacks to governmental officials are deductible unless the individual has been convicted of making the bribe or has entered a plea of not guilty or nolo contendere.

IRS OFFICIAL TAXPAYERS' GUIDE

Maybe there's a reason for all this.

Minorities, women, and the mentally challenged are strongly encouraged to apply.

JOB ANNOUNCEMENT PUT OUT BY THE UNITED STATES DEPARTMENT OF THE INTERIOR, NATIONAL BIOLOGICAL SURVEY

[My budget employees] are the kind of people that run over dogs. [Pause] I meant that in the best possible way.

REAGAN BUDGET DIRECTOR JAMES MILLER

Hairsplitting

Successfully wheedling your way out of tough spots requires true talent. A talent for hairsplitting. Hairsplitters like to distinguish between "this" (the bad thing they're being accused of) and "that" (the okay thing they did). Problem is, most of us can't see the difference. Take this theoretically critical distinction:

I DIDN'T ACCEPT IT. I RECEIVED IT.

RICHARD ALLEN, NATIONAL SECURITY ADVISOR TO PRESIDENT REAGAN, EXPLAINING THE $1,000 IN CASH AND TWO WATCHES HE WAS GIVEN BY TWO JAPANESE JOURNALISTS AFTER HE HELPED ARRANGE A PRIVATE INTERVIEW FOR THEM WITH FIRST LADY NANCY REAGAN

Perhaps the distinction escapes you? (Not to worry. Us, too.)

Still, intrepid hairsplitters keep enthusiastically splitting those hairs.

Staff members do not have chauffeurs. [They have] aides who drive.

LEWIS THURSTON, CHIEF OF STAFF FOR NEW JERSEY GOVERNOR THOMAS KEAN

WE DIDN'T TURN HIM DOWN. WE DIDN'T ACCEPT HIM.

PRESIDENT OF SPRINGDALE GOLF CLUB (PRINCETON, NEW JERSEY), EXPLAINING WHY A BLACK APPLICANT WAS REJECTED

I don't own an SUV. . . . The family has it. I don't have it.

SENATOR JOHN KERRY (D-MASSACHUSETTS)

The term "forced busing" is a misnomer, [because children] don't *have* to ride a bus, but only to arrive on time at their assigned schools.

BILL LANN LEE, CLINTON ASSISTANT ATTORNEY GENERAL CIVIL RIGHTS APPOINTEE

Halloween

October 31. A night when ghosts walk, witches fly, and vampires prowl for victims. Vampires like Dracula, probably the most famous of them all.

HOST: *Where does Dracula come from?*

CONTESTANT: *Umm . . . Pennsylvania.*

QUIZ SEGMENT ON THE VIRGIN RADIO MORNING SHOW

STEVE WRIGHT: *Which legendary bloodsucking creature was created by Bram Stoker?*

CONTESTANT: *The leech.*

BIG SHOW, BBC RADIO 2

Okay, maybe Dracula just isn't that popular anymore. This is probably why *new* horror shows on TV these days feature *new* truly terrifying monsters.

9:00: The Real Prince Philip

Continuing Channel 4's Halloween horror season

TELEVISION LISTING IN *THE GUARDIAN* (ENGLAND)

It's the night when kids dress up and go out for candy . . . or, uh, other things.

FOR TURNING TRICKS ON HALLOWEEN

SIGN IN COSTUME SHOP, HONG KONG

Remember, however, that Halloween means more than just dressing up or getting candy. It's a way of proving how *patriotic* you are!

God Bless America

Buy a pumpkin

SIGN OUTSIDE A CHURCH IN ATLANTA, GEORGIA

Happiness

What makes us happy? Philosophers have long pondered this question. Others find it easy to answer.

The toothbrush is an indispensable part of enjoying life. I brush my teeth every day. I have a wonderful time!

TOOTHBRUSH WRAPPER FROM JAPAN

THE JOY OF CHICKENS

THE BOOKSELLER MAGAZINE'S ODD TITLE OF THE YEAR IN 1980

TV executives think of themselves as *the* great purveyors of happiness.

Do you know what our suicide rate would be if we didn't have television? Do you know how much happiness I've brought to people who couldn't get out of the house but could watch *The Love Boat*?

PRODUCER AARON SPELLING

These media guys take their responsibility as purveyors of happiness pretty seriously.

We tried to make Jean-Michel Basquiat into an upbeat story, so we left out his death from choking on his own vomit.

PRODUCER OF THE FILM *BASQUIAT*, ABOUT THE RISE AND FALL OF THE DRUG ADDICTED ARTIST

Other people have what we may kindly call more complicated ideas about happiness.

Beauty is love made real, and the spirit of love is God. And the state of beauty, love and God is happiness. A transcendent state of beauty, love and God is peace. Peace and love is a state of beauty, love and God. One is an active state of happiness and the other is a transcendent state. That's peace.

PHILIPPINES' FIRST LADY IMELDA MARCOS, CAMPAIGNING FOR HER HUSBAND, FERDINAND MARCOS

But we leave it to an actress to zero in on the true meaning of happiness.

I feel my best when I'm happy.

ACTRESS WINONA RYDER

Headlines

Newspapers tell us what we need to know about the world; they teach us, they inform us, they keep us up-to-date on current affairs. Sometimes, though, when we read the papers, it seems that maybe we kind of knew it all already.

Sadness Is No. 1 Reason Men and Women Cry

OMAHA (NEBRASKA) WORLD HERALD

LIGHT MEALS ARE LOWER IN FAT, CALORIES

THE HERALD-DISPATCH (HUNTINGTON, WEST VIRGINIA; SOUTHERN OHIO; AND EASTERN KENTUCKY)

Or even if we didn't, we could probably have figured it out on our own.

Bible Church's Focus Is the Bible.

ST. AUGUSTINE (FLORIDA) RECORD

Some newspapers offer hard-hitting personal advice and commentary, which are equally valuable to the reader.

How We Feel About Ourselves Is the Core of Self-Esteem Says Author Louise Hart

BOULDER (COLORADO)
SUNDAY CAMERA

FREE ADVICE: BUNDLE UP WHEN OUT IN THE COLD

LEXINGTON (KENTUCKY)
HERALD-LEADER

Others don't hesitate to offer their take on controversial social topics.

Teen-Age Girls Often Have Babies Fathered By Men

THE SUNDAY OREGONIAN

Other newspapers, such as the world-class *New York Times*, are famous as being "papers of record" read by decision makers all over the world for their insightful articles.

Survey Finds Dirtier Subways After Cleaning Jobs Were Cut

THE NEW YORK TIMES

They could choose a higher-cost plan, which would cost them more, or a lower-cost plan, which would cost them less.

THE NEW YORK TIMES, ON HOW CLINTON HEALTH-CARE PLAN WOULD AFFECT A TYPICAL COUPLE

Penetrating insight isn't restricted to the *Times*.

Renewed Fighting Threatens Peace

OTTAWA (ONTARIO) *CITIZEN*

CHILDBIRTH IS BIG STEP TO PARENTHOOD

NEWSPAPER HEADLINE

Heaven

Is there a heaven? Many of us are pretty sure there is. And some of us can tell you exactly what it's like. And we do mean exactly.

> Heaven is a city 15,000 miles square or 6,000 miles around. One side is 245 miles longer than the length of the Great Wall of China. Walls surrounding Heaven are 396,000 times higher than the Great Wall of China and eight times as thick. Heaven has twelve gates, three on each side, and has room for 100,000,000,000 souls. There are no slums. The entire city is built of diamond material, and the streets are paved with gold. All inhabitants are honest and there are no locks, no courts, and no policemen.
>
> REV. DR. GEORGE HAWES OF HARRISBURG, PENNSYLVANIA

There is a little debate, however.

> Heaven is a place large enough to accommodate 299,900,000,000,000,000 souls with a mansion of 100 rooms each, 16 × 16 × 16.
>
> REV. DR. W. GRAHAM WALKER, SPEAKING AT THE HIGHLAND STREET CHRISTIAN CHURCH, MEMPHIS, TENNESSEE

Baseball fans should *really* like heaven . . .

Baseball will be taught in Heaven.

DR. JOHN HOWARD DIKASEN, SPEAKING BEFORE THE
UNIONTOWN, PENNSYLVANIA, KIWANIS CLUB

But before they get too excited:

There aren't any real leagues here, but old teams do get together quite often to give the crowds some excitement.

THE PURPORTED SPIRIT OF BASEBALL
GREAT BABE RUTH, SPEAKING FROM
HEAVEN, AS REPORTED IN *VOICES
FROM SPIRIT* MAGAZINE

Football fans might not find teams in heaven, but they'll find the whole setup reassuringly familiar.

The Kingdom of Heaven is like a football squad, which is assembled under a coach who formed it into a team that moved with such order and precision, in startling innovation, that it subdued all its opponents.

REV. LARRY CHRISTENSON, SERMON AT UNIVERSITY OF NOTRE
DAME FOOTBALL STADIUM

Okay. Heaven sounds great. And it's not as hard to get there as you might think, especially if you're open to using public transportation.

HAREWOOD CHRISTIAN DISCUSSION GROUP

We shall be meeting on Wednesday, 11th April when the subject will be "Heaven. How do we get there?" Transport is available at 7:55 P.M. from the bus stop opposite the Harewood Arms.

COLLINGHAM (ENGLAND) PARISH MAGAZINE

But how do you get *in*?

This is the gate of Heaven. Enter ye all by this door. (This door is kept locked because of the draft. Please use side entrance.)

ON A CHURCH DOOR

Help, Getting

We all need help from a professional from time to time. You know, like from those helpful people who work in telephone directory assistance:

CALLER TO INFORMATION, TRYING TO GET THE NUMBER FOR *THEATRE ARTS* MAGAZINE: *Could I please have the number of Theatre Arts?*

OPERATOR: *Sorry, but there's nobody listed by the name of Theodore Arts.*

CALLER: *It's not a person. It's a publication. I want Theatre Arts.*

OPERATOR *(speaking more loudly): I told you, we have no listing for Theodore Arts.*

CALLER *(getting frustrated): The word is Theatre. T-H-E-A-T-R-E.*

OPERATOR: *That is not the way to spell Theodore.*

And, of course, the folks in tech support are specially trained to answer any questions customers might have.

We need to make this output keyed, for some end user will put cable in wrong slut.

Also, if it happened that the cable just fitting in but there will be no funcation by this connection then it will caused some time to explain.

Pleas feel confront about this.

TECHNICAL SUPPORT E-MAIL REPLY

So is your friendly server at the local restaurant.

Customer: How long will the pancakes be?

Waiter: Not long. They're usually pretty round.

Help Wanted Ads

Anyone perusing the help wanted ads will notice that there's a job for everyone.

You've got low self-esteem?
Have we got some jobs for you.

NOW HIRING ALL SHI TS, FULL AND PART TIME

SIGN MISSING AN F, OUTSIDE A SUBWAY SANDWICH SHOP IN CORNELIOUS, NORTH CAROLINA

Now hiring losers.

MARQUEE NOTICE FOR HOT 'N NOW FAST-FOOD STORE THAT WAS LOOKING FOR "CLOSERS"

No qualifications? Why not try the U.S. Government?

Only unqualified applicants may apply.

Only applicants who do not meet standards will be considered.

TWO SEPARATE POSITION ANNOUNCEMENTS FOR THE U.S. FOREST SERVICE

If you prefer the private sector:

Restaurant Assistant Manager: Applicants with the necessary experience need not apply.

HELP WANTED AD

Or if a pleasant work environment isn't your cup of tea:

Finally, for those who are literally *dying* to get a job:

WANTED MAN TO BARBECUE.
Apply in person.
Renners Smoked Pic,
4249 Shallowford Rd.

AD IN CHATTANOOGA, TENNESSEE, NEWSPAPER

Outside Consultant Sought for Test of Gas Chamber

HEADLINE IN *PHOENIX* (ARIZONA) *REPUBLIC*

Are you a lively and stimulating teacher?

Do you enjoy working within a supportive and caring environment?

Are you happy working alongside dedicated and committed staff?

Are you challenged by articulate, perceptive and thoughtful children?

If the answers are YES, then this is the wrong school for you.

AD FOR TEACHER IN *THE REPORTER* (SAFFRON WALDEN, STANSTON, AND SAWSTON, ENGLAND)

Identity, Mistaken

It happens to the best of us. We meet someone we've met before and we just can't place the name or face. But some people are better (which is to say worse) at this than others.

Talent agents seem particularly prone to these mental lapses.

AGENT LEW GRADE: *Twenty-five is ridiculous for your work. I can get you forty. Who's your agent?*

ACTOR: *You are.*

AGENT PHIL GERSH, *after bumping into someone at Hollywood's Musso & Frank Grill: I'm very sorry, but I'm drawing a blank. Do I know you?*

DIRECTOR PHIL AARON: *I'm Phil Aaron. And you're Phil Gersh, my agent.*

Yes, it's a tough thing remembering people who are giving you 10 or 15 percent of their income! Or, for that matter, those who are keeping you from bodily harm.

VICE PRESIDENT DAN QUAYLE (EXTENDING HIS HAND DURING A CAMPAIGN STOP AT HARDEE'S): *I'm Dan Quayle. Who are you?*

WOMAN: *I'm your Secret Service agent.*

So let's learn a lesson from one poor soul: If you're not sure who someone is, just keep your mouth *shut.*

ENGLISH ARISTOCRAT:
Who is that ugly woman who just came in?

LORD NORTH:
Oh, that is my wife.

ARISTOCRAT: *Sir, I beg your pardon. I do not mean her. I mean that shocking monster who is along with her.*

LORD NORTH:
That is my daughter.

Instructions

We live in a world of rules, regulations, and instructions, all designed to make our lives easier and less confusing.

> **To Avoid Breakage, Keep Bottom on Top.**
>
> **Top Marked Bottom to Avoid Confusion**
>
> SIGN ON A CARTON

Many times, instructions are there to protect us, so we know exactly what to do in an emergency.

> **IN CASE OF FIRE, EVACUATE THE BUILDING.**
>
> **DO NOT USE STAIRWAYS.**
>
> **DO NOT USE ELEVATORS.**
>
> SIGN BY ELEVATOR IN THE FEDERAL RESERVE BANK BUILDING, BOSTON

Other times, they're written to make sure we get exactly what we deserve . . . sort of.

If combining a non-refundable fare with a refundable fare only the y/c/j-class half return amount can be refunded. After departure fare is refundable. If combining a non-refundable fare with a refundable fare refund the difference/if any/between the fare paid and the applicable normal BA oneway fare.

BRITISH AIRWAYS INSTRUCTIONS ABOUT TICKET CHANGES AND CANCELLATIONS

Some instructions assume a little too much. . . .

FILL IN THE CARD CLEARLY IN THE FOLLOWING LANGUAGES: CHINESE, ENGLISH, FRENCH AND SPANISH.

INSTRUCTIONS ON BACK OF IMMIGRATION FORM, CHINA

Parking for Blind Only

SIGN IN LAKEWOOD, COLORADO

PARKING

Other directives presume that we have a real way with tongue-twisting words.

[Call 911 and] say these words: "There has been a life-endangering emergency at the Department of Justice exercise facility."

STEP ONE OF A LIST OF INSTRUCTIONS POSTED IN THE JUSTICE DEPARTMENT'S OCCUPATIONAL HEALTH AND PHYSICAL FITNESS PROGRAM FACILITY (I.E., THE GYM)

Most often, though, instructions are spelled out clearly and succinctly. For example, concerned about how to sit down in a chair? The Seattle Police Department has helpfully provided tips for this procedure:

Take hold of the arms and get control of the chair before sitting down.

MEMO TO SEATTLE POLICE, AFTER TWO WORKERS FELL OFF THEIR ROLLING CHAIRS

Interviews, Broadcast

Interviews on TV and radio are a wonderful way for us to get firsthand information from interesting guests. But it takes a good interviewer to make for exciting broadcasting.

Good interviewers ask those tough, probing questions.

> ## Where were you first born?
>
> JOOLS HOLLAND, MUSICIAN AND INTERVIEWER

They know that the key to a good interview is to *listen*.

> **ATHLETE:** *I'm 43 now and have lost confidence through having so many setbacks.*
>
> **INTERVIEWER:** *And how old are you now?*
>
> ON-AIR INTERVIEW

They think on their feet and ask the questions we'd never think of.

> **INTERVIEWER EAMONN HOLMES:** *How long does London Fashion Week last?*
>
> **FASHION PUBLICIST:** *Um, a week.*
>
> GMTV (UK)

Granted, sometimes getting an interesting answer from interview subjects is tough . . .

> **HOST ROY WALKER:** *So you're a teacher's assistant. What do they do?*
>
> **CONTESTANT:** *Assist teachers.*
>
> CONVERSATION DURING A GAME SHOW

but most often, interviews are sheer poetry on the air.

> **RADIO SPORTSCASTER JIMMY HILL:** *But you said it should have been a goal.*
>
> **RADIO SPORTSCASTER TERRY VENABLES:** *No, I didn't. I said it should have been a goal.*
>
> **HILL:** *So you've changed your tune, then.*

Interviews, Job

Hundreds of books have been written on how to handle a job interview. They all have pretty much the same standard advice. So let's look at actual examples from actual job applicants to see how well they translated the advice into action.*

■ Open the interview by showing how excited you are about being there.

> I'm sorry I'm yawning. I usually sleep until my soap operas are on.

■ Quickly establish your burning interest in the job.

> Do you know of any companies where I could get a job I would like better than this one?

*ACTUAL INTERVIEW ANSWERS COLLECTED BY *FORTUNE* MAGAZINE AND VARIOUS HUMAN RESOURCE FIRMS, INCLUDING CALIPER, OFFICETEAM, ROBERT HALF ASSOCIATES, AND CHALLENGER AND GREY

What job am I applying for, anyway?

What is it that you people do at this company, anyway?

Why aren't you in a more interesting business?

■ Don't hide your failings—turn them into *positives!*

I would have been more successful if nobody would have snitched on me.

My resume might make it look like I'm a job hopper. But I want you to know that I never left any of those jobs voluntarily.

■ Ask the right sort of questions—ones that show you'll be a vital asset to the company.

What are the zodiac signs of all the board members?

Will the company move my rock collection from California to Maryland?

Would it be a problem if I'm angry most of the time?

WILL THE COMPANY PAY TO RELOCATE MY HORSE?

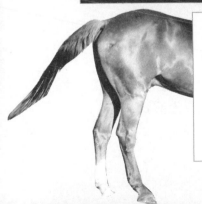

■ Better yet, make statements that will catch the interviewer's attention. Make sure to pause and let him or her catch the full impact of the statement.

I have no difficulty in starting or holding my bowel movement.

At times I have the strong urge to do something harmful or shocking.

I FEEL UNEASY INDOORS.

Sometimes I feel like smashing things.

I am fascinated by fire.

■ Show your "can do" attitude toward work.

WOULD ANYONE NOTICE IF I CAME IN LATE AND LEFT EARLY?

What does this company consider a good absenteeism record?

The job description mentions weekend work. Are you serious?

WILL MY OFFICE BE NEAR AN ICE MACHINE?

How many warnings do you get before you are fired?

You're FIRED!

■ If the interview is still going well, lob an interesting "personal" statement for the interviewer to ponder.

I never get hungry.

My legs are really hairy.

I had hemorrhoids from sitting at the desk all day, but I found that taking a walk after lunch really helped me.

■ Ask "probing" questions that show how you'll "fit in" with your coworkers.

HOW DO YOU DEFINE SEXUAL HARASSMENT?

WHAT ARE YOUR PSYCHIATRIC BENEFITS?

■ Take charge of the interview! Answer questions with clever "comeback" questions to show the interviewer you can think on your feet:

> **INTERVIEWER:** *Why do you want the job?*
>
> **JOB HUNTER:** *I'm here for a paycheck. Isn't everybody?*

INTERVIEWER: *Where do you see yourself in five years?*

JOB HUNTER: *How am I supposed to know? Isn't that your job?*

■ Finally, close the interview by making sure they'll remember you!

Introductions, Disastrous

Introducing people can be a risky thing. Sure, it seems easy. But stand in front of a group of people and something might go a little wrong.

Sometimes the one word that's on your mind, the one you *don't* want to say, comes out.

THIS COUNTRY NEEDS A SPEARCHUCKER, AND I THINK WE'VE GOT HIM UP ON THIS PODIUM.

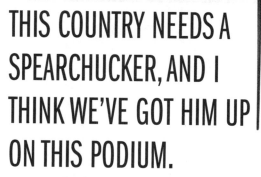

KENOSHA, WISCONSIN, MAYOR EUGENE DORFF, INTRODUCING ACTIVIST JESSE JACKSON (HE SAID LATER HE INTENDED TO SAY "STRAIGHT SHOOTER.")

Other times, you try a little too hard to
wow the audience . . .

**HERE NOW IS THE REVEREND
FATHER MCFADDEN—KNOWN
ALL OVER THE CITY, ALL OVER
THE COUNTRY, ALL OVER THE
WORLD AND ALL OVER THE . . .
ALL OVER THE . . . ER, AND
OTHER PLACES BESIDES.**

MEMBER OF BRITISH PARLIAMENT, INTRODUCING A
SPECIAL GUEST

. . . or you just get a little tongue-tied.

**[MY COLLEAGUE],
THE SENIOR
SENATOR FROM
JUNIOR.**

SENATOR HOMER CAPEHART
(R-INDIANA)

For some reason, introducing couples can be particularly dicey.

Ladies and gentlemen, it is my honor to introduce you to the governor of this great state, the Honorable John J. McKeithen and his lovely wife, Marjorie. Look how beautiful she is—every wrinkle in her face is glowing.

NEW ORLEANS MAYOR VIC SCHIRO, INTRODUCING THE GOVERNOR AND HIS WIFE AT A CITY COUNCIL MEETING

SPEAKING OF ANIMALS, HE MARRIED HIS WIFE, SUZANNE, WHEN HE WAS IN COLLEGE.

UTAH GOVERNOR MIKE LEAVITT, INTRODUCING SENATOR LARRY CRAIG (R-IDAHO)

Pros will tell you to just keep going with your intro. You'll get your point across . . . eventually.

My friends, it's with a great deal of pride that I present to you a president who wants to cut jobs—who wants to cut taxes to cut jobs—who wants—who wants to stop the regulations to cut the jobs . . .

POLITICIAN INTRODUCING PRESIDENT GEORGE H. W. BUSH TO AN AUDIENCE

HERE IS MISS MONICA DICKSON TO GIVE YOU ANOTHER TALK ON COCKING AND SNOOPING— I BEG YOUR PARDON—ON SHOCKING AND COOPING, ER, I'M SO SORRY—MISS MONICA DICKSON.

TELEVISION REPORTER LESLIE MITCHELL, ATTEMPTING TO
INTRODUCE A GUEST WHO WAS GOING TO TALK ABOUT
COOKING AND SHOPPING

Jocks, Dumb

Why is it that there is a dumb jock stereotype? We just can't figure it out.

Right now, I have the three C's: comfortable, confident, and seeing the ball well.

SEATTLE MARINERS OUTFIELDER JAY BUHNER

REPORTER: *Is your improved play due to your maturity?*

HOCKEY PLAYER JAY MILLER: *It's not so much maturity as it is growing up.*

Their coaches certainly show intellectual perspicacity.

PLAYER: *One of our players has real charisma.*

UNIVERSITY OF OKLAHOMA COACH: *What? Will he be okay by Saturday?*

REPORTER: *Do you think it's going to rain?*

FLORIDA STATE FOOTBALL COACH BILL PETERSON: *What do you think I am? A geologist?*

Maybe that comes from a true love of learning.

I'M REALLY HAPPY FOR COACH COOPER AND THE GUYS WHO'VE BEEN AROUND HERE FOR SIX OR SEVEN YEARS, ESPECIALLY OUR SENIORS.

OHIO STATE QUARTERBACK BOB HOYING, AFTER WINNING A BIG TEN TITLE

We can see the result in our college athletes:

REPORTER: *Can you compare studying at school with reading your football playbook?*

GREEN BAY PACKERS BACK CHRIS DARKINS: *The studying is a lot more words. The playbook is a lot more pictures.*

ASKED TO COMPARE HIS SCHOOL WORK AT THE UNIVERSITY OF MINNESOTA WITH STUDY AT FOOTBALL TRAINING CAMP

Justifications, Creative

Most people, when faced with an uncomfortable predicament, either tell the truth or tell a lie. But there are a few people who are more imaginative.

It wasn't a shark attack but a shark accident. More than likely he ran into [the swimmer's] leg and got it caught in his mouth.

JOE RUBIO, SOUTH PADRE ISLAND, TEXAS, TOWN SPOKESMAN EXPLAINING AWAY RUMORS THAT A WOMAN HAD BEEN ATTACKED BY A SHARK WHILE SWIMMING

This talent can be especially useful during, er, sticky situations.

[THE STAIN ON THE BLUE DRESS] COULD HAVE BEEN SPINACH DIP OR SOMETHING.

MONICA LEWINSKY, IN HER GRAND JURY TESTIMONY, COMMENTING ON THE SEMEN STAIN ON HER FAMOUS BLUE GAP DRESS

It's usually best practiced by those who have both ingenuity *and* bravado.

BRAZILIAN INVESTIGATOR: *Mr. Alves, how do you explain the money found in your bank account?*

JOAO ALVES, POLITICIAN ACCUSED OF EMBEZZLING MONEY: *It's my money.*

INVESTIGATOR: *But can you please explain to us how you made this kind of money?*

ALVES: *Easy. I won it all in lottery tickets. I won 125 times in the last two years.*

When they said, "Your sister is very ugly and very stupid," what they meant was, "Sir, I am afraid your sister is fairly attractive and ravishing." Korean words meaning "nice looking" are also synonymous with "ugly" and so is the word "smart" standing in for "stupid."

KOREAN LECTURER KIM YOUNG WHA, RESPONDING TO A VISITING TEACHER'S REMARK THAT HIS STUDENTS HAD TOLD HIM HIS SISTER WAS UGLY AND STUPID

The result: a justification that could, just possibly *could*, convince people it's true.

IT'S NOT TRUE [THAT THE CONGRESSMAN WAS SLEEPING DURING THE DEBATE]. HE WAS JUST TAKING A FEW MOMENTS FOR DEEP REFLECTION.

AIDE TO REP. MARTIN HOKE (R-OHIO), SEEN ON HOUSE FLOOR WITH EYES CLOSED DURING DEBATE

Maybe, if they're a little gullible, that is.

Legislation, Innovative

Lawmaking doesn't have to be dull. Take the problems of energy use and rising oil prices. Most legislators would come up with something boring, such as a price freeze. What does a truly *innovative* legislator suggest?

We should abolish January and February. If we then divide the fifty-nine extra days between July and August, we will cut our energy needs by about one-third through eliminating the coldest days of the year. Cold is largely a psychological matter. If people look at the calendar and see that it is July, they will be quite happy to turn the heat down.

OHIO STATE REPRESENTATIVE JOHN GALBRAITH

(Note: For some reason, the Ohio legislature never acted on this idea.)

Some innovative legislators get their new
and improved ideas from the public.

One of my constituents suggested we amputate trigger
fingers. The people are way out in front of the
politicians on the crime issue.

WASHINGTON STATE REPRESENTATIVE IDA BALLASIOTES

Yup, the people often lead the way,
innovationwise.

I see "hell" in "hello." It's
disguised by the o, but once you
see it, it will slap you in the face.

FLEA MARKET OPERATOR LEONSO CANALES OF KINGSVILLE,
TEXAS, ON HIS COUNTY-SUPPORTED CAMPAIGN TO CHANGE
THE WORD HELLO

The result?

HEAVEN-O!

NEW OFFICIAL WAY OF SAYING HELLO IN KLEBERG COUNTY,
TEXAS. THE LOCAL GOVERNMENT UNANIMOUSLY PASSED THE
ORDINANCE REPLACING HELLO.

Library Patrons

We can safely assume that people who go to libraries can read. But can they *think?* Mull over these general-knowledge questions asked of librarians.*

- Do you have books here?

- Do you have a list of all the books written in the English language?

- I have an emergency and I need the telephone number for 911.

- Can you tell me why so many famous Civil War battles were fought on National Park sites?

*AMERICAN LIBRARY ASSOCIATION'S *AMERICAN LIBRARIES* MAGAZINE, MOST STUPID QUESTIONS ASKED OF LIBRARIANS

· I was here about three weeks ago, looking at a cookbook that cost $39.95. Do you know which one it is?

· I got a quote from a book I turned in last week but I forgot to write down the author and title. It's big and red, and I found it on the top shelf. Can you find it for me?

· Do you have a list of all the books I've ever read?

· Which outlets in the library are appropriate for my hair dryer?

Logic,
Pentagon and

Logic is the ability to reason from facts and arrive at reasonable conclusions. Remember that "if A, then B" stuff in high school? Neither do we. So let's learn logic from the Defense Department!

First, the Defense Department's "If no A, then A" rule.

> ## THE FACT THAT THE INSPECTORS HAVE NOT YET COME UP WITH NEW EVIDENCE OF IRAQ'S WMD PROGRAM COULD BE EVIDENCE, IN AND OF ITSELF, OF IRAQ'S NONCOOPERATION.
>
> SECRETARY OF DEFENSE DONALD RUMSFELD, AFTER U.N. WEAPONS INSPECTOR HANS BLIX SAID THE INSPECTORS HAD FOUND NO "SMOKING GUNS"

Got that? Okay, now for the "A equals B, therefore A does NOT equal B" rule.

We have permitted our naval capability to deteriorate. At the same time we are better than we were a few years ago.

SECRETARY OF DEFENSE CASPAR WEINBERGER, ON THE UPS AND DOWNS OF THE U.S. NAVY IN 1982

Then there's the excessively logical "A equals A, so therefore A equals A."

WE'RE TRYING TO EXPLAIN HOW THINGS ARE GOING, AND THEY ARE GOING AS THEY ARE GOING.

SECRETARY OF DEFENSE DONALD RUMSFELD, AT A PENTAGON BRIEFING ON IRAQ

Maybe it takes a politician to aptly summarize the state of thought that's going on above.

What a waste it is to lose one's mind—or not to have a mind. How true that is.

VICE PRESIDENT DAN QUAYLE, ADDRESSING A UNITED NEGRO COLLEGE FUND AFFAIR AND GARBLING ITS SLOGAN: "A MIND IS A TERRIBLE THING TO WASTE."

Losing,
Sports and

L osing is, unfortunately, an integral part of sports.

There are always excellent— sometimes complicated— explanations for a loss.

> I thought we probably played this week like I thought maybe we could have played last week, and I didn't even think we could play that bad last week if we play like this.
>
> INDIANAPOLIS COLTS COACH TED MARCHIBRODA, WHEN HIS TEAM LOST TO THE SEATTLE SEAHAWKS AFTER WINNING THE PREVIOUS PRESEASON GAME

Sometimes the explanations aren't that complicated.

> [FIONA MAY] ONLY LOST OUT ON THE GOLD MEDAL BECAUSE NIURKA MONTALVO, THE SPANISH ATHLETE, JUMPED A LONGER DISTANCE THAN HER.
>
> SPORTSCASTER DAVID COLEMAN

Losing makes philosophers of people.

We lost because we didn't win.

SOCCER STAR RONALDO

EVEN NAPOLEON HAD HIS WATERGATE.

PHILADELPHIA PHILLIES MANAGER DANNY OZARK, COMMENTING ABOUT A PHILLIES' TEN-GAME LOSING STREAK

Some losers have that "never say die" ethos.

YOU KNOW, IF WE HADN'T GIVEN THEM THOSE FIRST FOUR TOUCHDOWNS, IT MIGHT HAVE BEEN DIFFERENT.

H. K. "COOTIE" REEVES, HOKES BLUFF (ALABAMA) HIGH SCHOOL FOOTBALL COACH, WHEN HIS TEAM LOST 53 TO 0 IN THE STATE DOUBLE A TITLE GAME

Then there are those who don't pull any
punches.

**REPORTER (AFTER THE
SAINTS HAD LOST):**
*What do you think
of the refs?*

**NEW ORLEANS SAINTS GENERAL MANAGER
JIM FINKS:** *I'm not allowed to comment
on lousy officiating.*

The key, of course, is identifying just
where things went wrong.

WE MADE TOO MANY
WRONG MISTAKES.

BASEBALL GREAT YOGI BERRA, EXPLAINING WHY THE
YANKEES LOST THE 1960 WORLD SERIES

And remember, hope springs eternal.

REPORTER: *How will you rebound from your
35-point loss?*

SEATTLE SUPERSONICS PLAYER SAM PERKINS:
We just have to maintain our consistency.

Nature, Love of

L et's look at a special breed of nature lovers: celebrities. They're *very* concerned about preserving the environment.

Sometimes they don't quite get it right.

> **CLEAN WATER IS ONE OF THE LEADING CAUSES OF DEATH IN THE WORLD.**
>
> SINGER JEWEL, TRYING TO EXPLAIN THE NEED FOR BETTER WATER-FILTRATION SYSTEMS

> *I have a great feeling for the soil. My brother is the leading conservationalist in the world, and I just love sitting on my bulldozer and experiencing nature.*
>
> GOLF STAR GARY PLAYER, ON HIS PLANS TO BUILD NEW GOLF COURSES IN FLORIDA

[The movie *Amazon*] takes place in the Amazon and what you realize is that this man has to make major choices, and he makes major mistakes instead of the right things, and through his mistakes he learns a lot of soulful things, and he actually corrects his inner life, which, of course, helps enhance his outer life, and through the whole process we learn about how sad it is that we have something called the Amazon forest and we're destroying it, and yet I say as an American-Canadian actress, it's sad what we're doing to [forests] in America.

ACTRESS RAE DAWN CHONG

Some celebrities love nature so much, they make huge sacrifices . . . like not wearing furs.

People don't know about the human part of me that really cares about the world. For instance, I don't know what I feel about wearing my furs anymore. I worked so hard to have a fur coat and I don't want to wear it anymore because I'm so wrapped up in the animals. I have real deep thoughts about it because I care about the world and nature.

SINGER DIANA ROSS

Others aren't sure they're ready for that big sacrifice.

I believe that mink are raised for being turned into fur coats and if we didn't wear fur coats those little animals would never have been born. So is it better not to have been born or to have lived for a year or two to have been turned into a fur coat? I don't know.

PLAYBOY BUNNY TURNED ACTRESS BARBI BENTON

We don't know, either. Maybe Barbi should ask a mink.

Newscasters, Stuttering

Newscasters are paid to read the news from a Teleprompter in a clear, commanding voice. Sometimes, though, they get a little tongue-tied . . .

At times, you almost want to sing along.

CONGRESSMAN JERRY HUCKABY WAS IN RAVEL TODAY TO SPEAK TO THE TA LOO TA LOO—TA LOO . . .

NEWSMAN, KTVE-TV, MONROE, LOUISIANA

Sometimes you can't help wondering if there's something Freudian underneath.

3 . . . 2 . . . 1 . . . There's a better than 50 percent chance the space shittle . . . [then, a minute later] Okay, ready . . . 3 . . . 2 . . . 1 . . . There's a better than 50 percent chance the space shittle . . .

TV NEWSWOMAN, DOING A TAPED STAND-UP PIECE ON THE SPACE SHUTTLE

Other times there's a certain rap-song quality.

Aides said the president is plotting his blitz to get those budget butts thruts but cuts.

TV NEWSWOMAN HELEN HOWARD

The rule generally is: If at first you don't succeed, try, try again. And again.

TAKE 1: Coast guard officials urge all of us to use extreme caution if we have to walk on frozen livers and lakes.

TAKE 2: With the warmer temperatures we've been experiencing so far this week, ice and livers . . .

TAKE 3: Coast guard officials urge all of us to use extreme caution when walking on ice-covered livers.

NEWSWOMAN, WTVG-TV, TOLEDO, OHIO

Take 1: How can a little groundhog in Punxsutawney, Mimme– Minnesota . . .

Take 2: How can a little groundhog in Punxsutawney, Penasot–

Take 3: How can a little groundhog in Punxsutawney, Penacil–

Take 4: How can a little groundhog in Punxsutawney, Penalsa-

TV NEWSWOMAN (MEANING TO SAY PUNXSUTAWNY, PENNSYLVANIA)

But if the right word just won't come out, your enterprising newsperson may choose to be innovative and use another word!

TAKE 1: A LITTLE GIRL'S CHWISTMAS . . . CHRISTMAS . . .

TAKE 2: A LITTLE GIRL'S CHWISH–DAMNIT!

TAKE 3: A LITTLE GIRL'S HOLIDAY WISH AND IT'S NOT FOR TOYS.

NEWSWOMAN, KGTV, SAN DIEGO, CALIFORNIA, DOING A TAPED STAND-UP SEGMENT

Alas, the new word sometimes doesn't sound so newscasterly.

The three-count federal indictment states that Davis and the three others conspired to purchase drug traffic ma traffic ma traffic ma–the thing that's used for drugs.

TV NEWSMAN ON AIR

Nudity

It seems that more businesses and people are urging everyone to be "naturalists."

> **Would the fans along the outfield please remove their clothes?**
>
> PA ANNOUNCER TEX RICKARDS, AT EBBETS FIELD, BROOKLYN, NEW YORK, AFTER FANS HAD HUNG THEIR COATS ON THE TOP OF THE OUTFIELD FENCE

And why not? There might well be an important historical precedent for nudity.

FATHER NUDIST: All over the world, ever since mankind began, the beneficent qualities of sunshine have impressed the minds of men. In darkest Africa, all of the natives are nudists. . . . You'll admit Benjamin Franklin was civilized.

REPORTER: Of course.

FATHER NUDIST: Well, Benjamin Franklin was a nudist.

ELYSIA, THE VALLEY OF THE NUDE, 1933

Being nude doesn't make you a less serious person.

We take the serious news as seriously as anyone else does. We just happen to be naked.

NEWS ANCHOR CARMEN RUSSO, *NAKED NEWS*

But before you rip off your clothes, remember, there are drawbacks . . .

THAT'S THE LAST TIME I'M GOING TO COOK IN THE NUDE.

CABLE TALK-SHOW HOST ROBIN BYRD, AFTER ACCIDENTALLY BURNING HER BREASTS ON A BAKING PAN

There are *strict* laws governing nudity.

Prohibited from sunbathing nude: Women with revolting, large, disfigured, flabby and oblong breasts

FROM A PROCLAMATION ISSUED BY GIOVANNI PETRILLO, MAYOR OF THE SMALL ITALIAN BEACH TOWN OF PANTELLERIA, PREVENTING CERTAIN WOMEN FROM SUNBATHING IN THE NUDE

And cops are great at catching nude law-breakers . . .

TV NEWSWOMAN, WTVD-TV, DURHAM, NORTH CAROLINA: *Residents appreciate the beauty of wooded West Durham, but what they don't appreciate is a nude man who stops and stares. What should they do?*

POLICEWOMAN: *They should just run away from him. Basically, try to get whatever kind of description that he has: facial description, his height and body size, anything that sticks out abnormally.*

. . . no matter *what* it takes . . .

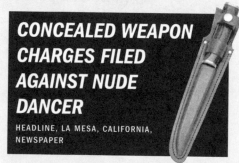

CONCEALED WEAPON CHARGES FILED AGAINST NUDE DANCER

HEADLINE, LA MESA, CALIFORNIA, NEWSPAPER

Observations, Clear

Some people have a knack for coming out with comments that really make you think. They cut through all the tough stuff and make complex subjects *understandable* even to us laypeople.

THE BEST WAY OF GETTING A JOB IS GETTING A JOB.

MITCH PEARLSTEIN, EXECUTIVE DIRECTOR, CENTER OF THE AMERICAN EXPERIMENT THINK TANK

You can't argue with that! And you can't argue with this either:

Our nation must come together to unite.

PRESIDENT GEORGE W. BUSH

Now, that's an interesting insight. Yes, there are those who are blessed, shall we say, with a facility for keen observation.

The car in front is definitely in the lead.

With half the race gone, there is half the race still to go.

We're now on the 73rd lap and the next one will be the 74th.

AUTO RACING COMMENTATOR MURRAY WALKER

If you make the right decision, it's normally going to be the correct one.

SOCCER PLAYER DAVE BEASANT

Sometimes these tautological observations sound almost Zen-like *(almost).*

Other times they don't.

UNTIL YOU HAVE HIM, YOU DO NOT HAVE HIM.

SECRETARY OF DEFENSE DONALD RUMSFELD, ON EXPECTATIONS THAT THE UNITED STATES WOULD SOON CAPTURE TERRORIST OSAMA BIN LADEN

Osama Bin Laden would never understand the joys of Hanukkah.

PRESIDENT GEORGE W. BUSH, SPEAKING AT A MENORAH-LIGHTING CEREMONY AT THE WHITE HOUSE

On The Other Hand . . .

Some people are masters at saying something and then, in the next breath, taking it all back.

> It really was the best field we've ever had. Except that it tore apart everywhere and kept changing colors.
>
> JOHN MARA, EXECUTIVE VICE PRESIDENT OF THE NEW YORK GIANTS, TALKING ABOUT THE $1.2 MILLION ARTIFICIAL TURF THAT WAS INSTALLED IN GIANTS STADIUM—AND DISINTEGRATED WITHIN MONTHS

Let's call these folks "masters of exception," since they use the word *except* a lot—right when they ease back on the conversational throttle. And speaking of throttles . . .

> *The lead car is absolutely unique, except for the one behind it, which is identical.*
>
> RACING COMMENTATOR MURRAY WALKER

Sometimes the masters of exception wind up "excepting" because they get carried away with rhetorical flourishes . . .

> IN A SENSE IT'S A ONE-MAN SHOW—EXCEPT THERE ARE TWO MEN INVOLVED, HARTSON AND BERKOVIC, AND A THIRD MAN, THE GOALKEEPER.
>
> SPORTSCASTER JOHN MOTSON

Other times they're victims of overstatement.

> **I came to Nantes two years ago and it's much the same today, except that it's completely different.**
>
> SPORTSCASTER BRIAN MOORE

It can be almost criminal! (Almost?)

> *I ROBBED FROM THE RICH, KIND OF LIKE ROBIN HOOD EXCEPT I KEPT IT.*
>
> CONVICTED THIEF, IN *THE SEATTLE* (WASHINGTON) *POST-INTELLIGENCER*

Opinions

Most of us have pretty strong opinions. But there are folks who seem a bit wary, let's say, of coming out and putting things right on the line.

That would be my opinion if I had an opinion, but as a member of my government, I have no opinion.

PAUL MARTIN, CANADIAN MINISTER OF EXTERNAL AFFAIRS, IN RESPONSE TO A QUESTION FROM TORONTO PRESS

Others have a "damn the consequences!" attitude and bravely and boldly state their opinions—which just happen to be extremely noncontroversial no matter how you look at them.

REPORTER: Do you support a smoking ban in bars?

NEW ZEALAND RESTAURANTEUR JUDITH TABRON: I think it . . . Well, let's face it, there is still the view that there could be other parties . . . as long as it is across the board, as long as we seriously have an across-the-board situation because I wouldn't want to see clubs with a different view here, because we all know, because we all know clubs can change their spots as we've seen in Australia.

And here's the ultimate in noncontroversiality.

I would expect things to go much as they are until there is some change.

SIR ANTHONY PARSONS, FORMER BRITISH AMBASSADOR IN THE MIDDLE EAST

Who could dispute that?!

Orders, Military

Anyone who's ever served in the Army—*any* army—knows that half the problems of service come from all those bureaucratic rules and regulations that superior officers foist on the lower ranks.

Sometimes it's kind of hard to follow orders.

ALL ICE CUBES WILL BE BOILED BEFORE USING.

U.S. ARMY OFFICIAL, ORDERING PREVENTIVE MEASURES DURING AN OVERSEAS TYPHOID EPIDEMIC

Or you wonder, *Why* are they asking us to do this?

This document did not concern you. Please erase your initials and initial your erasure.

U.S. ARMY PERSONNEL DEPARTMENT, FORT BAKER

Due to an administrative error, the original of the attached letter was forwarded to you. A new original has been accomplished and forwarded to AAC/JA [Alaskan Air Command, Judge Advocate office]. Please place this carbon copy in your files and destroy the original.

MEMO FROM THE ALASKA AIR COMMAND, FEBRUARY 1973

Sometimes it's all just a little too confusing . . . or a lot too confusing.

OPSDEP: Short for Operations Deputy. By JCS charter, the Army representative is the DCSOPS. However, the ADCSOPS (JA), who is the DEPOPSDEP, may act for the OPSDEP on all joint matters. The use of the term OPSDEP also includes DEPOPSDEP. OPSDEPs, or DEPOPSDEPs can approve papers for the JCS.

ARMY JOINT ACTIONS HANDBOOK

IT IS NECESSARY FOR TECHNICAL REASONS THAT THESE WARHEADS SHOULD BE STORED WITH THE TOP AT THE BOTTOM, AND THE BOTTOM AT THE TOP. IN ORDER THAT THERE MAY BE NO DOUBT AS TO WHICH IS THE TOP AND WHICH IS THE BOTTOM, FOR STORAGE PURPOSES, IT WILL BE SEEN THAT THE BOTTOM OF EACH HEAD HAS BEEN LABELED WITH THE WORD TOP.

BRITISH ADMIRALTY INSTRUCTION RE STORAGE OF WARHEADS AND TORPEDOES

Patriotism

Many Americans are proud patriots who don't hesitate to tell people so.

CANADIAN CUSTOMS OFFICER: *Do you have anything to declare?*

CINCINNATI REDS PITCHER STEVE FOSTER: *Sure. I'm proud to be an American!*

Some are so proud, they try to inject patriotism into what might be called an inappropriate topic.

Cold hands that turn red, white and blue may be patriotic, but they can be an early symptom of an auto-immune disease called scleroderma.

OPENING SENTENCE FROM A PRESS RELEASE FROM THE SCLERODERMA FOUNDATION, SENT TO NEWS AGENCIES JUST BEFORE JULY 4

We all know what America stands for . . . especially our political leaders.

You hear about constitutional rights, free speech, and the free press. Every time I hear these words I say to myself, "That man is a Red, that man is a Communist!" You never hear a real American talk like that.

JERSEY CITY, NEW JERSEY, MAYOR FRANK HAGUE

And they urge us, oh-so-eloquently, to fulfill our patriotic duties . . . no matter how onerous.

AND SO, IN MY STATE OF THE—MY STATE OF THE UNION—OR STATE—MY SPEECH TO THE NATION, WHATEVER YOU WANT TO CALL IT, SPEECH TO THE NATION—I ASKED AMERICANS TO GIVE 4,000 YEARS—4,000 HOURS OVER THE NEXT—THE REST OF YOUR LIFE—OF SERVICE TO AMERICA.

PRESIDENT GEORGE W. BUSH, ON HIS COMMUNITY SERVICE INITIATIVE

Yes, the bottom line for Americans is that we're *all* Americans and proud of it.

We're hoodlums—but we're *American* hoodlums!

ESCAPED CON (FRANK JENKS) DEALING WITH NAZIS, *SEVEN MILES FROM ALCATRAZ*, 1942

Percentages

Percentages are wonderful tools for backing up points and explaining things. The problem is you have to remember one key fact: It's all supposed to add up to 100% . . . isn't it?

> **THIS FIGHT IS GOING TO BE 90% MENTAL AND 50% PHYSICAL.**
>
> BOXING MANAGER LOU DUVA

> **Pitching is 80% of the game. The other half is hitting and fielding.**
>
> TEXAS RANGERS OUTFIELDER MICKEY RIVERS

You see, 100% is supposed to mean *all*. That seems to elude a few people, though.

> YOU GIVE 100% IN THE FIRST HALF OF THE GAME, AND IF IT ISN'T ENOUGH, IN THE SECOND HALF YOU GIVE WHAT'S LEFT.
>
> BASEBALL GREAT YOGI BERRA

And 50% (which, to refresh your memory, means half) is yet another problem-fraught concept.

> My dear Mr. Wallis, just read Sea Wolf. You told me in your office that it would be a 50–50 part (the role of Leach). I am sorry to say it is just the opposite.

ACTOR GEORGE RAFT, IN A WIRE TO PRODUCER HAL WALLIS

Twelve for 23. It doesn't take a genius to see that's under 50%.

SPORTS ANNOUNCER DICK VITALE

Then there are those who *do* seem to grasp the concept of percentages but go a little bit overboard.

> I'M ALL RIGHT. I'M GOOD ENOUGH TO BE HERE, BUT I'LL NEVER BE 100% AGAIN. WHO WILL BE? BUT 50 OR 75% OF ME IS BETTER THAN 100% OF 99.9 % OF PEOPLE ON THE PLANET.

WRESTLER GOLDBERG

Enough with the percentages already!

Philosophy, Celebrities and

You might be surprised at the depth of philosophical existential thought that emanates from a celebrity's brain. (Then again, perhaps surprise is not quite the correct word.)

When I get lonely, I want to be alone. I like to indulge in my loneliness so I can figure out that I'm not really lonely.

ACTRESS ALICIA SILVERSTONE

ELEVATOR PASSENGER: Where do you want to go?

MODEL CLAUDIA SCHIFFER: I don't know, I've never been there.

CONVERSATION WHEN SCHIFFER WALKED INTO THE OCCUPIED ELEVATOR, PRESSED A BUTTON THAT DIDN'T LIGHT UP BECAUSE THE FLOOR WAS UNOCCUPIED, THEN CONTINUED TO HOLD DOWN THE BUTTON

Sometimes celebrities grapple with the great ideas that have engaged such illustrious minds as Plato, Socrates, and Aristotle.

Other times, the ideas with which they grapple seem to have *eluded* Plato, Socrates, and Aristotle.

NOTHING MEANS NOTHING, BUT IT ISN'T REALLY NOTHING BECAUSE NOTHING IS SOMETHING THAT ISN'T.

PHILADELPHIA 76ERS PLAYER DARRYL DAWKINS, JUST BEFORE HE STARTED HOLDING TO HIS VOW OF SILENCE WITH SPORTSWRITERS

What would happen if you melted? You know, you never really hear this talked about that much, but spontaneous combustion? It exists! . . . [People] burn from within. . . . Sometimes they'll be in a wooden chair and the chair won't burn, but there'll be nothing left of the person. Except sometimes the teeth. Or the heart. No one speaks about this—but it's for real.

ACTOR KEANU REEVES

So, for a world view, why turn to Thomas Aquinas or Maimonides— when we can have Fiona Apple?

I'M A MESS AND YOU'RE A MESS, TOO. EVERYONE'S A MESS. WHICH MEANS, ACTUALLY, THAT NO ONE'S A MESS. KNOW WHAT I MEAN?

SINGER FIONA APPLE

Police

The police are there to protect us, and we know that most police officers are wonderful, smart, fine, upstanding, and competent officers of the law. But sometimes the police can seem maybe just a tad . . . *overzealous*.

CASUAL DRUG USERS OUGHT TO BE TAKEN OUT AND SHOT.

LOS ANGELES POLICE CHIEF DARRYL GATES, TO THE SENATE JUDICIARY COMMITTEE, REGARDING CASUAL USERS OF MARIJUANA AND COCAINE

[The exports include] thumbscrews and cattle prods, just routine items for the police.

COMMERCE DEPARTMENT SPOKESMAN, ABOUT A REGULATION ALLOWING THE EXPORT OF VARIOUS PRODUCTS ABROAD

And some may not be "up to speed" with all those complicated, pesky legal niceties in the Constitution.

> [Hijackers should be given] a rapid trial . . . with due process of law at the airport, then hanged.
>
> LOS ANGELES POLICE CHIEF EDWARD DAVIS

Sometimes police seem a little too cynical.

> **IF [BABIES] HAD ENOUGH STRENGTH TO PULL THE TRIGGER ON A GUN IF THEY HAD ONE, THEY'D USE IT. THEY'D KILL YOU RIGHT THERE.**
>
> ROBERT VERNON, ASSISTANT LOS ANGELES POLICE CHIEF, IN AN AUDIOTAPE FROM HIS SERIES "THE TRUE MASCULINE ROLE" RECORDED IN 1977 FOR THE GRACE COMMUNITY CHURCH, SUN VALLEY, CALIFORNIA

And we always liked babies! For that matter, some officers can be just a bit off the mark intellectually.

> CAN YOU HEAR ME? SQUEEZE ONCE FOR YES AND TWICE FOR NO.
>
> POLICE DETECTIVE QUESTIONING A WOUNDED OFFICER

Sometimes you've got to wonder: Just what kind of police department is my taxpayer dollar funding anyway?

Naked Romp
at Kinki Police
Academy

HEADLINE, *SOUTH CHINA MORNING POST*

Maybe the problem comes from the new types of training police recruits now undergo.

The police department wants young, aggressive men to consider a life in law enforcement. New recruits are given intensive training in handling of firearms, marksmanship, self-defense and finger painting.

PUBLIC-SERVICE MESSAGE READ ON-AIR AT A SMALL FM STATION IN MAINE

Umm . . . finger painting?

Political Correctness

Political correctness is about being
sensitive to the feelings of others.
Particularly of women and minorities.
It means being sensitive enough to, say,
blowtorch any snowman or snowperson
you happen to see. Immediately.

*The snowman is, of course,
white and invariably male. . . .
[His] ritual location in the semi-
public space of garden or field
imaginatively reinforces a spatial
social system, marking women's proper
sphere as the domestic-private and
men's as the commercial-public. . . . It
presents an image, however jocular, of
a masculine control of public space.*

ART HISTORIAN TRICIA CUSACK

Another tip: Never say *man* when you can say *person*.

Hello. This is Women in Entertainment. Our office will be personned again on Monday, the 24th of October.

WOMEN IN ENTERTAINMENT'S OUTGOING ANSWERING MACHINE MESSAGE

[MY DAUGHTER LOVES PLAYING] COWPERSONS AND INDIANS.

NOVELIST ANNE ROIPHE

Promote equality. In fact, go one step further.

My mother always made it clear to my sister and me that men and women were equal—if not more so.

VICE PRESIDENT AL GORE

Politicians, Crime-fighting

Despite today's crime-ridden world, we can all relax, knowing that our elected municipal officials are on top of things.

They know their cities so well that, in their inimitable way, they can zero in on the truth of the matter:

> **The streets are safe in Philadelphia; it's only the people who make them unsafe.**
>
> PHILADELPHIA MAYOR FRANK RIZZO

They point out the positive side. For example, maybe certain crimes are actually *good*!

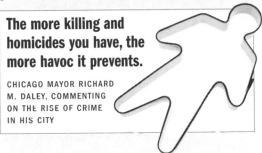

The more killing and homicides you have, the more havoc it prevents.

CHICAGO MAYOR RICHARD
M. DALEY, COMMENTING
ON THE RISE OF CRIME
IN HIS CITY

And, of course, they reassure us that things are actually much safer than you might think.

Outside of the killings, [Washington] has one of the lowest crime rates in the country.

WASHINGTON, D.C., MAYOR MARION BARRY

Well, maybe not.

Politicians, Overheard

Politicians have it tough. They have to be on their toes, not only when they see a microphone thrust in their faces, but also when they *don't* see that microphone. That's because sometimes microphones are around (and on) when a politician isn't quite as politic as usual.

Even about their bosses.

I WISH THAT COW WOULD RESIGN.

NORTHERN IRELAND OFFICE MINISTER RICHARD NEEDHAM, ON HIS CAR TELEPHONE, REFERRING TO PRIME MINISTER MARGARET THATCHER; OVERHEARD BY AN ELECTRONIC EAVESDROPPER AND REPORTED IN THE NEWS

Sometimes they weigh in with truly fascinating character insights about members of the media.

She has beeg breasts.

REPRESENTATIVE MARTIN HOKE (R-OHIO), ABOUT THE TV PRODUCER WHO HAD JUST PUT A LIVE MICROPHONE ON HIM

THERE'S ADAM CLYMER, MAJOR-LEAGUE A——HOLE FROM THE NEW YORK TIMES.

PRESIDENT GEORGE W. BUSH TO RUNNING MATE DICK CHENEY, IN A QUIET ASIDE THAT HAPPENED TO BE PICKED UP BY MICROPHONES

Once in a while, they very bluntly explain how they work (which tends to be very unlike what they say in public).

I have no scruples. What is good, we take advantage of. What is bad, we hide.

BRAZILIAN FINANCE MINISTER RUBENS RICUPERO, SPEAKING OFF-THE-CUFF DURING A BREAK IN A TELEVISION INTERVIEW TAPING, UNAWARE THAT THE SATELLITE FEED WAS STILL RUNNING (HE RESIGNED TWO DAYS LATER.)

Then there are times when they let us see their human side . . .

HATTIE, I'M HORNY.

FORMER ARIZONA GOVERNOR BRUCE BABBITT TO HIS WIFE, DURING HIS DEMOCRATIC PRESIDENTIAL CAMPAIGN

Poor, The

What is the difference between being rich and being poor?

> Perhaps the most significant difference between the rich and the poor is that the rich are likely to avoid interest charges on their credit-card bills while the poor might not be able to do so.
>
> AP WIRE SERVICE

Right. Very logical. And the poor face other problems besides mounting interest charges. Complicated problems.

> *The fundamental problem with being poor is that you don't have enough money.*
>
> ARTHUR LEVINE, PRESIDENT OF TEACHERS' COLLEGE, COLUMBIA UNIVERSITY

This is why some politicians realize that the poor need breaks. No, not food stamps (how outdated!), but. . .

> **I'm just tossing this out . . . but maybe we need a tax credit for the poorest Americans to buy a laptop.**
>
> HOUSE SPEAKER NEWT GINGRICH (R-GEORGIA)

Pop Tarts

"**P**op tart" used to refer only to a toaster pastry, which as we all know has no IQ. Now, however, the term is also used to refer to certain young pop singers who, as we also all know, *do* have IQs.

However, we're not going to venture to guess how high said IQs are.

SINGER TAYLOR HANSON *(during a "meet the fans" event): What day of the week is it?*

FAN: *Friday.*

HANSON: *All day?*

I'VE GOT TEN PAIRS OF TRAINERS. THAT'S ONE FOR EVERY DAY OF THE WEEK.
POP STAR AND MODEL SAMANTHA FOX

Ooookay. This is why many people think of pop tarts as not being the brightest pastries on

Originally my mother was Spanish, then she became a Jehovah's Witness.
SINGER GERI HALLIWELL
(FORMERLY OF SPICE GIRLS FAME)

the block. It doesn't help matters when reporters stump them with really *tough* questions.

REPORTER: *Are you attending the Cannes film festival this year?*

SINGER CHRISTINA AGUILERA: *I hope so. Where is it being held this year?*

REPORTER: *Now tell me, Britney, how do you feel about the meeting between George Bush and Tony Blair this week?*

SINGER BRITNEY SPEARS: *Who's Tony Blair?*

REPORTER: *He's the prime minister of Britain.*

SPEARS: *Well, he must be a very important person.*

But they fight back! Many, probably in an effort to shed that image of dumbness, do their utmost to be profound.

We try to convey to everybody that we're just learning just like everyone else. We're on this planet to be here, y'know, as humans.

SINGER CHRIS KIRKPATRICK, OF THE BAND 'N SYNC

> Sundance [Film Festival] is weird. The movies are weird. You actually have to think about them when you watch them.
>
> SINGER BRITNEY SPEARS

Other pop tarts seem to deliberately embrace the stereotype. (Well, we hope it's deliberate.)

YOU'VE DONE A NICE JOB DECORATING THE WHITE HOUSE.

SINGER JESSICA SIMPSON TO SECRETARY OF THE INTERIOR GALE NORTON, DURING A TOUR OF THE WHITE HOUSE

But perhaps we're being too harsh. After all, the way to pop stardom wasn't easy.

We were young and sacrificed a lot. I had to give up cheerleading, as did the others.

SINGER BEYONCE KNOWLES, ON HERSELF AND THE OTHER SINGERS IN DESTINY'S CHILD

Potatoes

For most people, potatoes are, well, . . . potatoes. But there might be more to this lowly tuber than you think.

LAURIE (MARIANNE GORDON): *But if this thing is actually killing people, then why is the mayor trying to keep it quiet?*

MORT (BILL OSCO): *Potatoes.*

LAURIE: *Potatoes?*

MORT: *Around here that means big money.*

THE BEING, 1983, THE ONLY MONSTER MOVIE SET IN IDAHO

People use the humble spud in colorful, *unique* ways in everyday speech.

You're such a little guy, though, very petite—like a potato.

Z-MOVIE CLASSIC *FOR YOUR HEIGHT ONLY*, 1979, FEATURING THE 3-FOOT-TALL HERO WENG-WENG, AKA AGENT 00

She beat me, and I ain't no slouch potato!

TENNIS STAR MARTINA NAVRATILOVA, AFTER LOSING AN EXHIBITION MATCH TO MONICA SELES

But, alas, potatoes are all too often over-looked. New and innovative potato-based products haven't set the world on fire.

Spudka

VODKALIKE ALCOHOLIC
BEVERAGE MADE BY
GROWERS OF IDAHO POTATOES

On the other hand, potato *sports* are taken very seriously.

British penalties for cheating in potato-growing contests are among the severest in the civilized world.

GABERONE (BOTSWANA) *STAR*

So, will the potato remain unloved, unsung and unacknowledged? As the old saying goes . . .

One doesn't know how many hot potatoes will appear over the horizon.

BRITISH MP DAVID MADEL

Power, Nuclear

People worry too much about nukes; at least, that seems to be the enlightened attitude of many government officials. Concerned about nuclear power? Well, fuggedaboudit!

If you set aside Three Mile Island and Chernobyl, the safety record of nuclear is really very good.

TREASURY SECRETARY PAUL O'NEILL

Even if we don't set those nuclear catastrophes aside, we should look at them, not as nuclear explosions, but as nicer-sounding things, like:

Nuclear power plant explosion: Rapid energetic dissembly

AS IDENTIFIED BY UTILITY OFFICIALS AT THREE MILE ISLAND NUCLEAR PLANT

Or how about this:

Releasing radioactive gas into the air: Controlled purging into the environment

AS IDENTIFIED BY OFFICIALS AT THREE MILE ISLAND
NUCLEAR PLANT

So don't spend your time worrying.
Workers at some nuclear power plants
certainly aren't. They're relaxed. *Really*
relaxed!

**NUCLEAR REGULATORY COMMISSION
INSPECTOR:**
*Were the two Dresden nuclear plant
operators sleeping on the job?*

**JOHN HOGAN, COMMONWEALTH EDISON
SUPERVISOR OF NEWS INFORMATION:**
*It depends on your definition of
asleep. They weren't stretched out.
They had their eyes closed. They were
seated at their desks with their heads
in a nodding position.*

So, yes, of course we can trust our alert nuclear workers to keep things safe.

NRC: Fuel rods mistakenly stored in safe place

GREENWICH (CONNECTICUT) *TIME*

And if something really bad happens, no problemo!

Actual meltdown takes three to five days, and that's certainly enough time to evacuate Long Island.

POLITICIAN GEORGE KOOP, LEGISLATIVE CANDIDATE IN
SUFFOLK COUNTY (LONG ISLAND, NEW YORK), IN SUPPORT
OF A LOCAL NUCLEAR POWER PLANT

So maybe we shouldn't be surprised to see headlines like this.

Area Man Wins Award for Nuclear Accident

NEWSPAPER HEADLINE

Predictions, Bad

When we want to know what the future will bring, we turn to top experts, highly trained people who can sniff out future trends before they've even started! So let's take a look at some old predictions and see how our crack experts fared.

Some predictions never quite seemed to get off the ground.

We stand on the threshold of rocket mail.

U.S. POSTMASTER
GENERAL ARTHUR
SUMMERFIELD, 1959

Experts were correct that women would enter the workforce. But to us, they seemed a bit off on what these working women would look like.

> Brain work will cause her to become bald, while increasing masculinity and contempt for beauty will induce the growth of hair on her face. In the future, therefore, women will be bald and wear long mustaches and patriarchal beards.
>
> PROFESSOR HANS FRIEDENTHAL OF BERLIN UNIVERSITY, ON THE EVOLUTION OF WOMEN AFTER THEIR BEING GRANTED HIGHER EDUCATION AND VOTING RIGHTS

Judge for yourself!

Experts also seemed a little too optimistic about the uses of old underwear.

> By 2000 . . . discarded paper table "linen" and rayon underwear will be bought by chemical factories and converted into candy.
>
> SCIENCE DIGEST, 1967

They thought housework would get easier—
and wetter.

> When [the housewife of 2000]
> cleans house she simply turns the
> hose on everything. Why not?
> Furniture (upholstery included),
> rugs, draperies, unscratchable
> floors—all are made of synthetic
> fabric or waterproof plastic. After
> the water has run down a drain in
> the middle of the floor (later
> concealed by a rug of synthetic
> fiber), [she] turns on a blast of hot
> air and dries everything.
>
> *POPULAR MECHANICS*, 1950

And unless we've missed something . . .

> # Nuclear-powered vacuum cleaners will probably be a reality in ten years.
>
> BUSINESSMAN ALEX LEWYT, PRESIDENT OF LEWYT CORP.
> VACUUM CLEANER COMPANY, IN *THE NEW YORK TIMES*, 1955

Presidency, the Clinton

The Clinton years were a rich source of—how shall we say it?—*vivid* metaphors.

Bidding has already started for her [Monica Lewinsky's] blow-by-blow account.

CAPITAL FM NEWS

Has Monica Lewinsky blown it for the President?

TV NEWSCASTER SCOTT CHISHOLM

SENIOR REPUBLICANS CERTAINLY EXPECTED THE PRESIDENT TO COME CLEAN OVER MISS LEWINSKY.

RADIO NEWSCASTER BRIDGET KENDALL

It just couldn't be helped. Even foreign diplomats dipped their oar . . . uh, well, you know . . .

I have the honor to give to the President of U.S.A., uh, an instrument of sex.

A FOREIGN DIGNITARY PRESENTING A SAXOPHONE TO PRESIDENT BILL CLINTON

Sometimes, we didn't know what to think when we read the papers . . .

At other times, we did know what to think but didn't want to go there . . .

There's a little bit of Bill Clinton inside all of us.

EDITORIAL, *SIKH MESSENGER* MAGAZINE (ENGLAND)

There had been rumors of a semen-stained dress six months earlier . . . the White House lawyers could not help worrying what else would leak out.

LONDON *SUNDAY TIMES*

The President may have been oblivious to it all.

The president was somewhat mystified as to why there was no mention of him in the 3 October 1995 article in the *Arkansas Democrat Gazette* entitled "Sex Can Wait plan gets $200,000 grant."

MEMO FROM CLINTON ADVISER HAROLD ICKES TO SECRETARY OF HEALTH AND HUMAN SERVICES DONNA SHALALA

Press Conferences

Press conferences enable journalists to get answers to questions—and so keep the news-hungry public fully informed.

Yes, press conferences offer valuable insights into newsworthy events.

GENTLEMEN, I HAVE NOTHING TO SAY. ANY QUESTIONS?

HOCKEY PLAYER PHIL WATSON TO REPORTERS

REPORTER: *Do you know to what extent the U.S. and Colombia are in fact cooperating militarily now, in terms of interdiction efforts?*

PRESIDENT GEORGE H. W. BUSH: *Well, I—Yes, I know that.*

REPORTER: *Can you share that with us?*

BUSH: *No.*

REPORTER: *Why not, sir?*

BUSH: *Because I don't feel like it.*

JUST BEFORE BUSH WAS GOING TO ATTEND A DRUG SUMMIT IN COLOMBIA

I HAVE NOTHING TO SAY. AND I'LL ONLY SAY IT ONCE.

TORONTO MAPLE LEAFS COACH FLOYD SMITH

With controversial subjects, we get a clear understanding of how our politicians *really* feel.

My position on Vietnam is very simple. And I feel this way. I haven't spoken on it because I haven't felt there was any major contribution that I had to make at the time. I think that our concepts as a nation and that our actions have not kept pace with the changing conditions, and therefore our actions are not completely relevant today to the realities of the magnitude and the complexity of the problems that we face in this conflict.

NEW YORK GOVERNOR NELSON ROCKEFELLER, WHEN ASKED FOR HIS POSITION ON THE VIETNAM WAR. (WHEN A REPORTER FOLLOWED UP WITH A QUESTION ASKING WHAT HE MEANT, ROCKEFELLER ANSWERED, "JUST WHAT I SAID.")

Often we're surprised at the eloquence of our public leaders.

> As I said already, they have conducted themselves in the last two or three years, much more discri–er, discree–discri–uh, with greater prudence and discretion than we have because it is, uh, I—I've forgotten what the question was.
>
> SENATOR J. WILLIAM FULBRIGHT (D-ARKANSAS), TRYING TO SMOOTHLY ANSWER A REPORTER'S QUESTION

And they most certainly encourage journalists to ask those probing questions that they know they can answer.

REPORTER: *Mr. Secretary, has anyone asked you the whereabouts of Mr. Molotov?*

SECRETARY OF STATE DEAN RUSK: *No. No one has asked me that question. You can if you want to.*

REPORTER: *Well, sir, where is Mr. Molotov?*

RUSK: *I haven't the faintest idea.*

UPON RUSK'S RETURN FROM A MOSCOW SUMMIT

Press Secretaries

A press secretary is a trained professional who gets up in front of a group of reporters and answers difficult questions— all in the name of making his boss look good.

Wait . . . did we say he *answers* questions?

I would feel that most of the conversations that took place in those areas of the White House that did have the recording system would in almost their entirety be in existence, but the special prosecutor, the court, and, I think, the American people are sufficiently familiar with the recording system to know where the recording devices existed and to know the situation in terms of the recording process, but I feel, although the process has not been undertaken yet in preparation of the material to abide by the court decision, really, what the answer to that question is.

NIXON PRESS SECRETARY RON ZIEGLER

They know how to come out with inarguable statements . . .

Democrats did very well in Democratic primaries.

CLINTON PRESS SECRETARY DEE DEE MYERS

Some of our friends are for it. Some of our friends are against it. And we're standing with our friends.

CLINTON PRESS SECRETARY MIKE MCCURRY, EXPLAINING WHETHER OR NOT PRESIDENT CLINTON WOULD VETO A BILL CURBING SECURITIES LAWSUITS

And many of them are experts at developing warm relationships with the press.

IF YOU TOOK OFF ALL YOUR CLOTHES AND SAT ON MY FACE, I MIGHT TELL YOU.

PETER FREYNE, PRESS SECRETARY TO THE GOVERNOR OF VERMONT, TO A FEMALE REPORTER WHO WAS ASKING QUESTIONS

Who'd you sleep with to get your job?

JON PECK, PRESS SECRETARY TO FLORIDA GOVERNOR BOB MARTINEZ, TO A FEMALE REPORTER

Products

There's nothing new under the sun, or so goes the old saying. We take exception to this, however. If you read advertisements, you'll learn that there *are* a lot of new things out there—or rather, new twists on old products.

Some products are ones you've seen before . . . but they've been remarketed to appeal to a brand-new customer group

Others are *enhanced,* if you will—a standard product with an unexpected, er, note.

Some are modern, high-tech versions of old standbys.

Super
Soft
Computerized
Socks

AD FOR AN INDIAN PRODUCT

And then there are those products that probably no one would want to buy . . .

BLEMISHES AVAILABLE
SELECTED SIZES &
COLOR $90

AD IN THE *NEW HAVEN* (CONNECTICUT) *REGISTER*

. . . never ever—no matter what a bargain it is.

20 TOILET ROLLS, HARDLY
USED, XMAS BARGAIN

CLASSIFIED AD IN THE BARROW (ENGLAND)
NORTH-WEST EVENING MAIL

Proverbs

There's nothing like a time-honored proverb to get your point across. You know, like:

If you give a person a fish, they'll fish for a day. But if you train a person to fish, they'll fish for a lifetime.

VICE PRESIDENT DAN QUAYLE, AT A JOB TRAINING CENTER IN ATLANTA, CELEBRATING THE 10TH ANNIVERSARY OF THE JOB TRAINING PARTNERSHIP ACT

Okay, let's rephrase that. There's nothing like a time-honored proverb to get your point across . . . providing you *know* the proverb. For some people, this seems to be a bit of a problem.

It's been feast or fathom for Jose.

JOE CARTER, BLUE JAYS WORLD SERIES HERO TURNED TV ANALYST, ON SLUGGER JOSE CANSECO'S CARFER WITH THE BLUE JAYS

Even so, you *usually* can get the gist of what they're driving at.

THAT WAS THE NAIL THAT BROKE THE COFFIN'S BACK.

VILLANOVA BASKETBALL COACH JACK KRAFT, ON LOSING A KEY PLAYER DURING THE LAST MINUTES OF A TIGHT GAME

Rome wasn't born in a day.
MILWAUKEE BRAVES SHORTSTOP JOHNNY LOGAN

I'm speaking off the cuff of my head.
CALGARY CITY COUNCILLOR JOHN KUSHNER

But sometimes it's nearly impossible (particularly when carrots get into the act) . . .

I can see the carrot at the end of the tunnel.
SOCCER PLAYER AND MANAGER STUART PEARCE

. . . (or sheep).

I just don't happen to belong to that branch of the sheep family that will follow a bellwether over a precipice.
REP. JOHN ASHBROOK (R-OHIO)

A lot of people get snagged on the details.

It's all water under the dam.

CALIFORNIA ANGELS
MANAGER LEFTY PHILLIPS

There are too many cooks in the fire.

ANTHONY BRADENTHALER,
ORGANIZER OF OREGON'S
CENTENNIAL CELEBRATION

And a lot of people seem to get stuck on two sayings in particular. Why they're tough to remember escapes us, but . . .

We'll cross that bridge when we fall off it.

CANADIAN PRIME
MINISTER LESTER
PEARSON

or rather . . .

LET'S JUMP OFF THAT BRIDGE WHEN WE COME TO IT.

TORONTO MAYOR ALLEN LAMPORT

But maybe we're being too picky.
As they say:

Don't cut off your nose yourself.
BASEBALL GREAT CASEY STENGEL

I don't want to cut anybody else's nose off to spite our face.
COMMENTATOR, ABC-TV, AUSTRALIA

After all, haven't we all mangled a cliché at one time or another? Maybe we should keep that old admonition in mind:

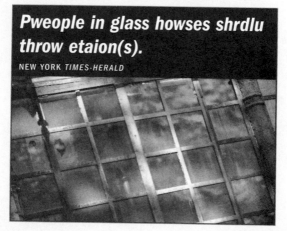

Pweople in glass howses shrdlu throw etaion(s).
NEW YORK *TIMES-HERALD*

Public Speaking

Public speaking ranks as one of the most stressful things a person can deal with. It shouldn't be that tough, though, when you think about it. It's just a matter of taking it step by step.

To begin with, as one of our former presidents succinctly put it:

> **When a man is asked to make a speech, the first thing he has to decide is what to say.**
>
> PRESIDENT GERALD FORD

What insight! The next thing you have to decide upon is how to open your speech. Many people start with a unifying comment, something that says, "I'm just like you." (This isn't as easy as it sounds.)

> VICE PRESIDENT DAN QUAYLE, BEGINNING A SPEECH AT THE OPENING OF AN APOLLO 11 ANNIVERSARY CELEBRATION:
>
> *My fellow astronauts . . .*

> AL SMITH, GOVERNOR OF NEW YORK, ADDRESSING THE INMATES OF SING SING PRISON:
>
> *My fellow convicts . . .*

Others prefer starting with a light joke as an icebreaker. Audiences just love that . . . or so it would appear.

American businessman is beginning his speech with a joke. I am not certain why, but all American businessmen believe it is necessary to start speeches with jokes. [Pause] He is telling the joke now, but, frankly, you wouldn't understand it, so I won't translate it. He thinks I am telling you the joke now. [Pause] The polite thing to do when he finishes is to laugh. [Pause] He is getting close. [Pause] Now! [Audience laughs and gives speaker standing ovation.]

JAPANESE TRANSLATOR TRANSLATING AN AMERICAN BUSINESSMAN'S SPEECH IN JAPAN (AFTER THE SPEECH, THE EXECUTIVE TOLD THE TRANSLATOR, "YOU ARE THE FIRST TRANSLATOR WHO KNOWS HOW TO TELL A GOOD JOKE.")

Next it's on to the meat of a speech. Here's where you present all those important points you want to get across.

> [A]nd there are the two major promises he has not been able to keep. And those are the promises to put more Americans back to work and the second promise is to, uh, [pause] what is that second promise?
>
> SECRETARY OF STATE JAMES BAKER

If you're the forgetful type, like Mr. Baker, it helps to have a printed copy of what you intend to say. But be careful.

> **Ladies and gentlemen, it is a great pleasure to be with you today. For immediate release only.**
>
> SENATOR JOSEPH MONTOYA (D-NEW MEXICO) AT A DINNER SPEECH IN ALBUQUERQUE, HAVING RUSHED IN LATE AND READING STRAIGHT FROM HIS PRESS RELEASE

A well-written speech should be one that is made for reading aloud. Rhetorical flourishes are helpful. You'll find yourself really getting into the rhythm of your words . . .

Remember Lincoln, going to his knees in times of trial in the Civil War and all that stuff. You can't be. And we are blessed. So don't feel sorry for—don't cry for me, Argentina.

PRESIDENT GEORGE H. W. BUSH, IN A CAMPAIGN SPEECH

Finally, end with a rousing pronouncement— an "up" note.

We have a firm commitment to NATO, we *are* a part of NATO. We have a firm commitment to Europe. We *are* a part of Europe.

VICE PRESIDENT DAN QUAYLE

And there is no doubt in my mind—not one doubt in my mind—that we will fail.

PRESIDENT GEORGE W. BUSH, IN A STIRRING SPEECH ABOUT THE FIGHT AGAINST TERRORISM

Questions,
Job Interview

We all know those basic questions you're always asked in job interviews: "Where do you see yourself in five years?" "Why do you want this job?" and, of course, the other old regulars.*

· So which Star Trek do you prefer, Old Series or Next Generation?

· Are you a dog person, a cat person, or a canary person, or do you like fish?

· Would you be willing to convert to the Amish religion? They are our main customers and they buy more easily from one of their own.

· You're not a terrorist, are you?

· If we hire you, would you be willing to stay as your current gender and agree not to have a sex-change operation?

· Can you go 8 hours without leaving your desk to go to the bathroom?

· How do you feel about intense verbal abuse?

---

*INTERVIEW QUESTIONS COLLECTED BY VARIOUS HUMAN-RESOURCE FIRMS

Quotations

People who talk to the press or public a lot know that one of the best ways to make a point is to quote someone else's words. It's effective for good reason: There are so many great sayings that are truly *unforgettable*.

> **As Francis Bacon said, some books are to be . . . What the hell did he say?**
>
> NEWSCASTER, CKTV, REGINA, SASKATCHEWAN, CANADA

You people are exemplifying what my brother meant when he said in his inaugural address, "Ask what you can do for . . . uh . . . do not ask what you can do . . . uh . . . ask not what you can do for your country but"— Well, anyway, you remember his words.

ATTORNEY GENERAL ROBERT KENNEDY

They can lend historical perspective to political points of view.

Just remember the words of Patrick Henry: "Kill me or let me live."

FLORIDA STATE FOOTBALL COACH
BILL PETERSON, IN A HALFTIME PEP
TALK TO HIS TEAM

YOU READ WHAT DISRAELI HAD TO SAY. I DON'T REMEMBER WHAT HE SAID. HE SAID SOMETHING. HE'S NO LONGER WITH US.

SENATOR ROBERT DOLE (R-KANSAS), WHEN
ASKED ABOUT THE CLINTON SEX SCANDAL,
TRYING TO EXPLAIN HOW HE KEEPS HIS
PRIVATE LIFE AND PUBLIC LIFE SEPARATE

Movie lines, in particular, resonate.

> **Cheered by their words and with an altogether more positive attitude to boxing . . . I found myself recalling the words of Marlon Brando in _On the Waterfront_, "I could have been a bartender."**
>
> _LOOK JAPAN_, AN ENGLISH-LANGUAGE MAGAZINE IN TOKYO

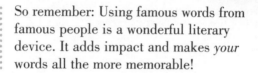

So remember: Using famous words from famous people is a wonderful literary device. It adds impact and makes *your* words all the more memorable!

> **Asked his conception of the Navy's role in a future war, Morrison picked up his book. "As certain as night succeeds the day, without a decisive navoin oiniou oiuiouiouoo ing definitive," he read. "Know who wrote that?"**
>
> _THE PATRIOT LEDGER_ (QUINCY, MASSACHUSETTS)

Er, actually, we don't.

Reading

It seems that people just don't read much anymore. Maybe everyone's watching too many movies . . .

HOST ANNE ROBINSON: *In Tolkein's Lord of the Rings trilogy, the third and final book is called "The Return of the" what?*

CONTESTANT: *Jedi.*

THE WEAKEST LINK

HOST ANNE ROBINSON: *Which character narrates all but four of the Sherlock Holmes books?*

PLAYBOY PLAYMATE CONTESTANT: *The Pink Panther.*

THE WEAKEST LINK

. . . or television?

HOST ANNE ROBINSON: In which H. G. Wells novel does an inventor travel in a machine of his own making?

CONTESTANT: *The Simpsons.*

THE WEAKEST LINK

Maybe they're relying too much on the, er, knowledge of bookstore clerks . . .

CUSTOMER: I'm looking for a copy of *Mein Kampf.*

BOOKSELLER: Is that the author?

CUSTOMER: No, it's German for *My Struggle*. It's by Hitler.

BOOKSELLER: Hitler who?

CUSTOMER: Are you serious?

BOOKSELLER (raising eyes in pained look): Look, I don't know *every* author in the world.

Or maybe their minds are still filled with children's classics?

HOST ANNE ROBINSON:
FOR WHICH BOOK DID SALMAN RUSHDIE WIN THE BOOKER PRIZE?

CONTESTANT:
THE WIND IN THE WILLOWS

THE WEAKEST LINK

HOST ANNE ROBINSON:
Who wrote *Cat on a Hot Tin Roof*?

CONTESTANT: Dr. Seuss.

THE WEAKEST LINK

Well, maybe not . . .

**HOST RICHARD
DAWSON:
Real or fictional,
name a famous
Willie.**

**CONTESTANT:
Willie the Pooh.**

FAMILY FEUD

HOST: Who killed Cock Robin?

**CONTESTANT: Oh, god. I didn't even know
he was dead.**

AUSTRALIAN GAME SHOW *THE AFTERNOON PROGRAMME QUIZ*

Religion,
Business and

Religion can be, um, a financial *blessing* for some businesses, from television to retail.

Of course, there can be some problems.

> ## You mean they've scheduled Yom Kippur opposite *Charlie's Angels*?
>
> NOTED TV PROGRAMMER FRED SILVERMAN, WHEN TOLD THAT YOM KIPPUR FELL ON A WEDNESDAY

The key is to approach religion in the proper reverential spirit.

PUT THEM SIDE BY SIDE AND OUR JESUS IS BETTER THAN THEIR JESUS.

CBS TELEVISION CEO LESLIE MOONVES, COMMENTING ON HIS NETWORK'S AND NBC'S COMPETING MINISERIES ABOUT JESUS

Feeling guilty about your sweet tooth? Well, thank God for minty fresh TESTAMINTS from America. These truly heavenly confectionaries are wrapped in verses from the scriptures. They have proved such a success that the range has been expanded to include sugar-free mints, seasonal tins (Christmas and Easter) and "promise pops" (each comes with a scripture verse on a peel-off sticker).

AD IN *TIME OUT* MAGAZINE

IT LOOKS LIKE AN ORDINARY CRUCIFIX, BUT ONE TUG WILL SET IT OFF. AND IT'S LOUD.

TONY McCARTHY, SPOKESMAN FOR AVON SILVERSMITHS, LTD., DISCUSSING THE COMPANY'S CRUCIFIX THAT COMES WITH A BUILT-IN ALARM

Even sweepstakes companies have gotten into the act—although we think they might be aiming a little too high.

God, we've been searching for you. What an incredible fortune there would be for God! Could you imagine the looks you'd get from your neighbors? But don't just sit there, God.

PART OF A LETTER FROM AMERICAN FAMILY PUBLISHERS, SENT TO GOD AT THE BUSHNELL ASSEMBLY OF GOD IN BUSHNELL, FLORIDA (THE LETTER STATED THAT GOD WAS A FINALIST FOR THE $11 MILLION TOP PRIZE.)

Resumes

Job experts all agree: your resume is your "ticket" to job-hunting success.*

A good resume sells you, the job hunter. Resume experts recommend that you begin your resume with an "objective."

OBJECTIVE:
My goal is to be a meteorologist. But since I have no training in meteorology, I suppose I should try stock brokerage.

OBJECTIVE:
To have my skills and ethics challenged on a daily basis.

OBJECTIVE:
10-year goal: Total obliteration of sales and federal income taxes and tax laws.

And make sure you remember that word *objective*.

OBJECTION:
To utilize my skills in sales.

*ACTUAL RESUMES COLLECTED BY VARIOUS HUMAN RESOURCES FIRMS

Always keep things brief and to the point:

While I am open to the initial nature of an assignment, I am decidedly disposed that it be so oriented as to at least partially incorporate the experience enjoyed heretofore and that it be configured so as to ultimately lead to the application of more rarefied facets of financial management as the major sphere of responsibility.

Next comes your educational background. Strive for accuracy.

Education: B.A. in Loberal Arts.

I have a bachelorette degree in computers.

Some of you may want to highlight your rather *extensive* educational background.

EDUCATION: College, August 1880–May 1984

Completed 11 years of high school.

Don't just list your schools. Highlight your academic accomplishments!

Finished eighth in my class of ten.

Graduated in the top 66% of my class.

Now it's time to summarize key points of your work background. Remember, you want to impress prospective employers!

Instrumental in ruining entire operation for a Midwest chain operation.

EXPERIENCE: WATERED, GROOMED, AND FED THE FAMILY DOG FOR YEARS.

PREVIOUS EXPERIENCE: Self-employed— a fiasco.

Extensive background in public accounting. I can also stand on my head!

Excellent memory; strong math aptitude;
excellent memory; effective management
skills; and very good at math.

And be sure to high-light any special skills you have.

Exposure to German for two years, but many words are inappropriate for business.

I am quick at typing, about 25 words per minute.

ENGLISH (FLUENT)

LISTED AS LANGUAGE PROFICIENCY ON THE RESUME OF
MELVIN SEMBLER, U.S. AMBASSADOR TO ITALY

Of course, some people have more skill than others.

Typing speed: 756 wpm

You may want to include reasons why you left your last job. Remember: Keep it positive!

> **REASON FOR LEAVING LAST JOB: The owner gave new meaning to the word *paranoia*. I prefer to elaborate privately.**

> REASON FOR LEAVING LAST JOB:
> They insisted that all employees get to work by 8:45 A.M. every morning. Could not work under those conditions.

And always include pertinent personality traits that show you're the one they should hire.

> I have become completely paranoid, trusting completely no one and absolutely nothing.

> *I PROCRASTINATE, ESPECIALLY WHEN THE TASK IS UNPLEASANT.*

My ruthlessness terrorized the competition and can sometimes offend.

List references, as well—if you have any.

REFERENCES:

None. I've left a path of destruction behind me.

Finally, show a bit of yourself, special interests you may have that tell the employer: *This* is the person I want to hire!

PERSONAL INTERESTS: Donating blood— 14 gallons so far

Rich, The

The rich are different from you and me. First off, they have a pretty different view of what being rich really *is*.

> ## DON SIMPSON HAD NO MONEY. MAYBE $30 MILLION AT THE MOST. THAT'S NOTHING.
>
> EX-PRODUCER JON PETERS, QUOTED IN *BUZZ WEEKLY* (HE LATER TOLD *THE* NEW YORK *DAILY NEWS* HE DIDN'T SAY THIS, ADDING, "I'D NEVER PUT DON SIMPSON DOWN, HE'S A SWEET GUY.")

And many of them get a little coy (or perhaps we should say "cloying") when it comes to discussing their wealth.

> ## I'D RATHER NOT TALK ABOUT MONEY. IT'S KIND OF GROSS.
>
> ACTRESS AND MULTIMILLIONAIRE BARBRA STREISAND, NOT TALKING ABOUT WHAT SHE WAS PAID TO DIRECT AND STAR IN *THE MIRROR HAS TWO FACES*

Of course, rich people are fully aware of how lucky they are. Heck, even if they just inherited it, they *deserve* to be rich, don't they?

ALLY HILFIGER (daughter of designer Tommy Hilfiger and star of *Rich Girls*): Yo, we're so fortunate. Like, I thank f——ing God—excuse me, Lord, I'm sorry to use your name in vain—I feel like I do not deserve all of this.

JAIME GLEICHER (Hilfiger's friend and costar of *Rich Girls*): Ally, you deserve it because you're not fixated on it and you appreciate it. It's not like, "Oh, back in Mustique, this is my house, blah, blah, blah." You don't take it for granted.

UNIDENTIFIED THIRD GIRL: Do you guys believe in past lives?

HILFIGER: Yes, I do.

GLEICHER: Like, Ally, I feel like you will be a child of Mustique because you love it and you love the sea.

HILFIGER: Yeah, or I would be a tree. I would be a tree.

GIRL: I feel like we're all old souls, though. Maybe we were just really good in our past lives.

ON AN EPISODE OF REALITY SHOW *RICH GIRLS*

But if you're envious of people with money, remember that the grass is always greener on the other side.

There's no way to make everybody rich. I don't even know if it's worth the trouble because the life of a rich person, in general, is very boring.

BRAZILIAN PRESIDENT FERNANDO HENRIQUE CARDOSO, RUNNING FOR REELECTION, IN A 1998 SPEECH IN THE PARQUE ROYALE SLUM OUTSIDE RIO DE JANEIRO

Don't you feel better now?

Royalty

There's a cachet about royalty, particularly the British royals. They're so sophisticated.
They always know *exactly* what to say at any social occasion.

HOW DO YOU KEEP THE NATIVES OFF BOOZE LONG ENOUGH TO PASS THE TEST?

PRINCE PHILIP, TO A SCOTS DRIVING INSTRUCTOR

You didn't manage to get eaten, then?

PRINCE PHILIP, TO A STUDENT WHO HAD SPENT THE YEAR IN PAPUA, NEW GUINEA

Their table manners are *impeccable*.

I didn't find [Prince Charles] stiff at all. He's very relaxed at the table, throwing his salad around and stuff.

SINGER MADONNA, AFTER HAVING DINNER WITH PRINCE CHARLES AT HIGHGROVE

Many royals lead somewhat unusual lives.

The Queen has stayed four times as Mr. Farish's private guest at his Kentucky stud farms, lending him a social cachet in return for which he waived his stud fees for his royal visitor.

THE GUARDIAN (ENGLAND)

Of course, just because they're royals doesn't mean they don't have their problems. But the press tends to "hush things up."

Unfortunately some royalty face recognition problems.

WEAKEST LINK HOST ANNE ROBINSON: What "H" was the hereditary disease carried by Queen Victoria?

CONTESTANT: Syphilis.

The Duke of Edinburgh arrived in an RAF helicopter today to embark on his first official visit to the Irish Republic. The drunk was later to attend a function with Mrs. McAleese at Dublin Castle.

WOLVERHAMPTON (ENGLAND)
EXPRESS & STAR

HOST BEN STEIN:
After his abdication, King Edward VIII of England became know as the Duke of where?

CONTESTANT: Duke of Earl

TV QUIZ SHOW *WIN BEN STEIN'S MONEY*

Here comes the Royal Family now. The automobile has now stopped, a member of the RCMP is opening the car door—oh, there's the King—he's stepping out, followed by her Majesty Queen Elizabeth, nattily attired in a silver coat. Mr. King is now shaking hands with the King and introducing Mr. Queen to the King and Queen and then Mrs. Queen to the Queen and King. They are now proceeding up the steps to the well-decorated City Hall, the King and Mr. King together with the Queen being escorted by Mrs. Queen. The King has now stopped and said something to Mrs. Queen and goes to Mrs. Queen and the Queen and Mr. King and the Queen laughed jovially. The King leaves Mr. King and goes to Mrs. Queen and the Queen and Mr. King follow behind. . . .

A CANADIAN BROADCASTING CORPORATION RADIO ANNOUNCER DOING HIS BEST TO DELIVER A COHERENT ON-THE-SPOT REPORT OF THE 1939 VISIT OF KING GEORGE VI AND HIS WIFE TO WINNIPEG AND OF THEIR MEETING WITH THE CANADIAN PRIME MINISTER, MACKENZIE KING, AND THE MAYOR OF WINNIPEG, JOHN QUEEN, AND HIS WIFE

Scripts, Film

Great films are full of great lines that everyone remembers and quotes. This is not about them.

Pity the poor actor or actress who has to deliver lines such as:

> **THOSE DEAD PEOPLE SURE ARE SMART!**

MAN TRYING TO ESCAPE FROM ZOMBIES, WHEN HE DISCOVERS THAT THE ZOMBIES HAVE TAKEN THE DISTRIBUTOR CAP OUT OF THE ESCAPE VEHICLE, *DEAD PIT,* 1989

> It's great to eat under an open sky, even if it is radioactive.

RICK BALDWIN (FRANKIE AVALON), ENJOYING A PICNIC WITH THE FAMILY IN POST-NUCLEAR-HOLOCAUST LOS ANGELES, *PANIC IN THE YEAR ZERO,* 1962

> **And what are little boys made of? Is it snakes and snails and puppy dog tails? Or is it brassieres! And corsets!**

NARRATOR, *GLEN OR GLENDA,* 1952

NATIVE WOMAN: *I just saw the Tabonga!*

WITCH DOCTOR: *Well, how do you know it was Tabonga?*

NATIVE WOMAN: *Because it looked like a tree and it had eyes and hands!*

NATIVES FORECASTING DOOM IN THE RADIOACTIVE-TREE-GONE-BERSERK HORROR FILM *FROM HELL IT CAME*, 1957

THERE IS A HERD OF KILLER RABBITS HEADING THIS WAY!

PANICKY SHERIFF WARNING TEENAGERS AT THE DRIVE-IN OF IMPENDING DOOM, *NIGHT OF THE LEPUS*, 1972

Sometimes actors even have to learn a foreign language (or Hollywood's *conception* of a foreign language). The results are even worse.

TICOORA: Mahorib! Stop this. What will Liongo think?

MAHORIB: Ogah yogo magia.

TICOORA : Harango!

MAHORIB : Hanama!

TICOORA : Penagullem!

MAHORIB : No. White devils kill.

CONVERSATION BETWEEN TICOORA (LOIS HALL) AND THE WITCH DOCTOR MAHORIB (FRANK LACKTEEN), *DAUGHTER OF THE JUNGLE*, 1949

And as for romantic dialogue . . .

You will be welcome in Zukuru! The head man's locust bean cakes— they'll be your locust bean cakes! His fermented buffalo milk will be your fermented buffalo milk.

SHEENA (TANYA ROBERTS) DECLARING HER UNDYING LOVE FOR VIC CASEY (TED WASS), *SHEENA*, 1984

When I'm sitting here with you, I don't even think about slime people. . . .

HERO TO HEROINE, *THE SLIME PEOPLE*, 1963

Yes, it can be tough for actors and actresses. Even the big ones.

Kokumo can help me find Pazuzu!

FATHER LAMONT (RICHARD BURTON) NAMING THE AFRICAN HEALER WHO WILL HELP HIM FIND THE EVIL ONE, *EXORCIST II: THE HERETIC*, 1977

Self-identity

Most of us know who we are. We've mastered the not-so-difficult art of telling people our names, first and last, with at least some degree of accuracy. For some reason, however, many newspeople haven't.

ANCHORMAN: Good evening. I'm Mark Bedor.

ANCHORWOMAN: And I'm Nancy Silva. Oh, excuse me, I'm Corinna Russ. Nancy Silva is on vacation.

ON THE NIGHTLY NEWS, KCPM-TV, CHICO, CALIFORNIA

Good evening. I'm Kevin Galant. I'm Ken Newfeld, pardon me.

NEWSCASTER, CKTV NEWS SERVICE, REGINA, SASKATCHEWAN, CANADA

Sometimes they do just fine with their first names, but they have last-name issues.

Hi, folks, I'm Jerry Gross. No, I'm not, I'm Jerry Coleman.

SAN DIEGO PADRES ANNOUNCER JERRY COLEMAN

Good evening, I'm Beverly Thomas. No, I'm Beverly Luckett.

NEWSWOMAN, WXVT-TV, GREENVILLE, MISSISSIPPI

Prince Charles may have more serious identity problems . . .

His comments followed claims that the Prince has been secretly Mrs. Parker-Bowles for more than a decade, and as often as once a week.

LONDON EVENING GAZETTE

but they're nothing like those of Mrs. Plonk, or is that Clonk? . . . or Blonk?

Information wanted as to the whereabouts of Mrs. J. O. Plonk (Blonk) wife of J. O. Plonk (Clonk).

AD IN A CHINESE NEWSPAPER

Selling Out

It's easy to be cynical about people who make megabucks. You know, the ones who get multimillion-dollar contracts for acting or playing ball *and* sell out to the big corporations.

But they don't see themselves as sellouts. As far as they're concerned, it's most *definitely* not about the money. No, sir.

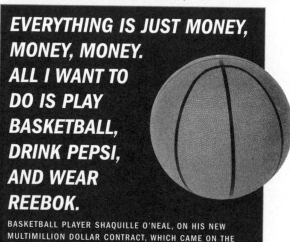

EVERYTHING IS JUST MONEY, MONEY, MONEY. ALL I WANT TO DO IS PLAY BASKETBALL, DRINK PEPSI, AND WEAR REEBOK.

BASKETBALL PLAYER SHAQUILLE O'NEAL, ON HIS NEW MULTIMILLION DOLLAR CONTRACT, WHICH CAME ON THE HEELS OF HIS PEPSI AND REEBOK ENDORSEMENT DEALS

See, it's really about *values*.

> # I COULD HAVE PAID OFF MY DEBTS A LOT QUICKER, BUT I ONLY DID THINGS I ACTUALLY BELIEVED IN MYSELF, LIKE CRANBERRY JUICE LITE.
>
> DUCHESS OF YORK SARAH FERGUSON, EXPLAINING HER CAREER AS AN ADVERTISING SPOKESPERSON

Of course, there are the big names who will never be tainted. They'll *never* be asked to do a product endorsement.

PRESIDENT OF THE REPUBLIC OF GEORGIA EDUARD SCHEVARDNAZE, TASTING COKE AT A NEW COCA-COLA BOTTLING PLANT JUST OPENING IN THE CAPITAL CITY, TBILISI:

It's just like Pepsi-Cola!

Shakespeare, Enduring Impact of

William Shakespeare. When it comes to writing, he's a biggie. As one informed and literate politician put it:

> ## SHAKESPEARE IS OUR GREATEST LIVING WRITER.
>
> BRITISH POLITICIAN DAVID MILLIBAND, DURING A RADIO INTERVIEW

Well, no. That's not quite right. Some people don't think he's the greatest writer. (Oh, and some—most of us, actually, probably virtually *all* of us—also think he's dead.) One thing is certain, though: Shakespeare was most definitely a great writer. Who among us can't quote some of his more famous lines?

HOST CRAIG STEVENS: *We're looking for a four-letter answer here. Shakespeare said that this by any other name would smell as sweet.*

CONTESTANT: *Soap?*

ON THE GAME SHOW
BRAINTEASER, CHANNEL 5, UK

Er . . . okay. Well, who among us doesn't know his plays?

Now I know how Shakespeare felt when he said, "Alone at last."

DON PORTER (TROY DONAHUE)
TO PRUDENCE BELL (SUZANNE PLESHETTE), IN *ROME ADVENTURE*, 1962

MOVIE MOGUL HARRY COHN: *I want a speech that every person in the audience will recognize immediately.*

SCREENWRITER: *You mean like Hamlet's soliloquy?*

COHN: *No! No! I mean something like "To be or not to be."*

HOST ANNE ROBINSON: William Shakespeare wrote seven plays about Kings of England who all shared the same name. What name?

CONTESTANT: Oh. . . . I don't have an answer . . . Ralph?

THE WEAKEST LINK

DJ: Who wrote Hamlet?

CALLER: Um, Macbeth.

DURING A RADIO CALL-IN CONTEST (CAPITAL GOLD, UK)

Never mind. Let's accept that Shakespeare is well known. So well known, in fact, that his name pops up in ordinary—and not so ordinary—conversation.

Did she have a Shakespearean section?

TORONTO MAYOR ALLAN LAMPORT, ON HEARING ABOUT AN ACQUAINTANCE WHO HAD JUST HAD A BABY

Spelling

Spelling *is* important, which is why newspapers sponsor spelling bees (which they might consider entering themselves).

Unfortunately, though, even with bees, it seems that spelling is rapidly becoming a lost art. This is why politicians feel strongly about helping educate the youth of America.

KEA Spelling Bee: Elevin Kentucky Students compete for the state championship

TV LISTING FROM A KENTUCKY NEWSPAPER

Tudors Needed

REP. JIM BACCHUS (D-FLORIDA), IN A LETTER TO OTHER REPRESENTATIVES "LOOKING FOR VOLUNTEERS TO TUTOR UNDERACHIEVING HIGH SCHOOL STUDENTS"

Of course, it would be simpler if the politicians themselves were better at spelling.

May our nation continue to be the beakon of hope to the world.

PRINTED MESSAGE INSIDE MARILYN AND DAN QUAYLE'S 1989 CHRISTMAS CARD

Yet, for all the problems, some people still do know how to spell.

CUSTOMER: How do you spell "Internet America"? Is there a space between "inter" and "net"?

TECH SUPPORT: No space between "inter" and "net." It's spelled normally.

CUSTOMER: Okay. A-M-E-R-I-C-K?

TECH SUPPORT: That's A-M-E-R-I-C-A.

CUSTOMER: I-C-K???

TECH SUPPORT: 'A' as in apple

CUSTOMER: There's no 'K' in apple!

CALL TO A COMPUTER
TECH-SUPPORT STAFFER

And newspapers remain vigilant! They try to snag all of those spelling mistakes and set an example for their readers.

Yesterday we issued an "Apology Notice" apologising for a printing error which led to the current posters for our range of HB Ice Cream being accidentally printed upside down.

Due to an oversight by our advertising agency the word "apology" was spelled incorrectly and read "apology."

ERRATUM NOTICE IN AN AD IN THE *IRISH TIMES*

Okay, sometimes they're a bit too vigilant.

During the five-and-a-half-month scam, the fraudsters regularly spelt the word "sinccrely" as "sincerely" and "forty" was mlspelt "forty".

Police alerted banks across the country to look out for such mispelt letters.

TRAVEL WEEKLY

Spontaneity

When something is spontaneous, it isn't planned. Or that's what we thought. Maybe we've been wrong all this time. . . .

> ## Beijing Plans Spontaneous Celebration
>
> HEADLINE, *THE TIMES* (UK)

Yes, it's true: When it comes to governmental types, spontaneity isn't exactly spontaneous.

It makes sense. If something unplanned happens, something

> ## The spontaneous rally will begin at 1:45.
>
> MIKE MURPHY, ADVISER TO LAMAR ALEXANDER IN HIS BID FOR THE 1996 REPUBLICAN PRESIDENTIAL NOMINATION

could go wrong. So politicians and their ilk opt for *prefab* spontaneity. That way, they can make sure that a "spontaneous" photo op looks good. (Why, they even suggest the best footage!)

> **She's going to be shoveling mud. Then she'll wipe the sweat from her brow, like this. Make sure you get that shot, all right?**
>
> NATHAN NAYLOR, VICE PRESIDENT AL GORE'S PRESS SPOKESMAN, BRIEFING NETWORK TELEVISION CREWS RIGHT BEFORE TIPPER GORE ARRIVED ON THE SCENE IN HONDURAS TO "HELP" CLEAN UP THE DEVASTATION CAUSED BY HURRICANE MITCH

And they can make sure that they've got a "spontaneous" answer to a pesky question.

REPORTER: Okay, what's the price of milk?

PRESIDENTIAL CANDIDATE STEVE FORBES: A dollar eighty-nine here, and two dollars and sixty-nine in New Jersey. It's one ninety-nine in New Hampshire.

AFTER THE MULTIMILLIONAIRE CANDIDATE WAS ACCUSED OF BEING OUT OF TOUCH WITH REGULAR MIDDLE-CLASS PEOPLE AND THEIR "POCKETBOOK" PROBLEMS

Sports, Insider Insights

If you want to understand a sport, you've got to talk to the players or their coaches. That's the whole idea behind locker-room interviews. You can get real "insider's" insights.

> **Better teams win more often than the teams that are not so good.**
>
> TORONTO MAPLE LEAFS COACH TOM WATT

You can learn how coaches strategize. (Be careful—it can get technical.)

> **We're not going to win if we don't score.**
>
> DETROIT RED WINGS HEAD COACH DAVE LEWIS, AFTER THE RED WINGS WERE SHUT OUT BY TAMPA BAY

You can learn all about what makes a winning streak.

> When it's going, it just kind of goes, and when it's not going, it kind of stops.
>
> SEATTLE SEAHAWKS COACH MIKE HOLMGREN

Or how a football defensive player really views his role.

Defensively, it's important for us to tackle.

DENVER BRONCOS LINEBACKER KARL MECKLENBURG, EXPLAINING HIS TEAM'S SUPER BOWL STRATEGY

You can learn how coaches look at individual players and positions, and hear their fascinating observations.

> You have to have a catcher because, if you don't, the pitch will roll all the way back to the screen.
>
> BASEBALL GREAT CASEY STENGEL

You can even learn to tell a seasoned sports broadcaster by the level of his commentary. He should sound just like the players and coaches, of course!

YOU CAN'T KNOCK IN RUNS IF THERE'S NO ONE ON BASE.

YANKEES BROADCASTER JOHN STERLING, DURING AN ALCS PLAYOFF GAME

Stars,
Confessions of

Celebrities love to share personal information about themselves with their adoring public. Sometimes, though, they get a little too . . . forthcoming. Or are we the only ones who think so?

I'm holding so much water now, I have a backside that looks like a cauliflower. And other parts of my body resemble strange vegetables like squashes or things like that.

ACTRESS KATE WINSLET, DISCUSSING HER NEW VEGETARIAN DIET

I didn't feel well earlier. That's why I fit into this dress. I was actually in the toilet all day.

ACTRESS JENNIFER LOPEZ, WHO WAS WEARING A VERY TIGHT DRESS AT A PREMIERE PARTY

What lovely images! And, of course, they can't help but share their insights on having a child.

When I got through with the twin pregnancy, my abdominal skin was such that I had to fold it up and then stick it in my pants.

ACTRESS CYBILL SHEPHERD

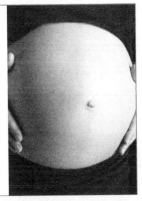

Statistics

According to the old saying, there are lies, damned lies, and statistics. But we feel this is unfair. Statistics can be terribly illuminating. . . .

They can underscore fascinating facts that most of us never knew.

> Statistics show that teen pregnancy drops off significantly after age 25.
>
> COLORADO STATE SENATOR MARY ANNE TEBEDO (R-COLORADO SPRINGS)

> **More than half (55 percent) of women undergraduates are female.**
>
> *ABOUT WOMEN ON CAMPUS*, NEWSLETTER PUBLISHED BY THE NATIONAL ASSOCIATION FOR WOMEN IN EDUCATION, REPORTED IN *CHRONICLE OF HIGHER EDUCATION*

For some context, consider these numbers from the same year, as reported by the *Cleveland Plain Dealer:* 91 percent of clergy were men, 92 percent of engineers were men, 90 percent of men were dentists.

YORK (PENNSYLVANIA) *DAILY RECORD*

Wow . . . think about all those dentists!

Sometimes statistical results do seem unbelievable.

Users of The Club are 400% less likely to have their car stolen.

COMMERCIAL FOR THE CLUB, AN AUTOMOTIVE ANTITHEFT DEVICE, WBZ, BOSTON

Why, you may ask, are statistics so problematic? Let's take a quick look at a key definition, which might clear things up.

Analysis of variance, Statistics: A procedure for resolving the total variance of a set of varieties into component variances, which are associated with various factors affecting the variates.

DEFINITION IN *THE AMERICAN COLLEGE DICTIONARY*

Tastefulness, TV Broadcasting and

Television has been called "the vast wasteland." We aren't sure why. It sure can't be due to the *programming*, can it?

> Okay, our focus: Are babies being bred for satanic sacrifice? Controversial to say the least. Unbelievable to say the least. Disgusting to say the least. We'll be right back.
>
> TALK SHOW HOST GERALDO RIVERA, LEADING INTO A COMMERCIAL BREAK

Tonight you'll be looking at some horrible scenes and meeting some horrible people.

GERALDO RIVERA, INTRODUCING HIS TV SPECIAL *MURDER: LIVE FROM DEATH ROW*

We are told, Tommy, and this may come as a surprise to you, that you have a 13-year-old son who is watching this program right now, who has just been told that you are his father and that you are a murderer.

GERALDO RIVERA TO DEATH ROW INMATE TOMMY ARTHUR, IN PRISON IN ALABAMA FOR KILLING HIS WIFE'S SISTER

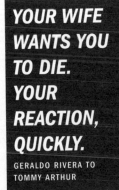

YOUR WIFE WANTS YOU TO DIE. YOUR REACTION, QUICKLY.

GERALDO RIVERA TO TOMMY ARTHUR

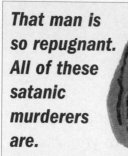

That man is so repugnant. All of these satanic murderers are.

GERALDO RIVERA, DISCUSSING CHARLES MANSON

Some programmers feel that there's been too much "dumbing down" for audiences. So they're aiming for more intellectual fare.

[Our new talk show] is not going to be "My sister is sleeping with my father." It's going to be "My sister is sleeping with my father, but they're both interested in the Middle East."

TALK SHOW HOST NICKY CAMPBELL ON HIS NEW SHOW

So if you're concerned about the future of television, we're here to tell you not to worry! TV shows will keep coming up with the same high-quality product they've been broadcasting for years.

Celebrities will be shown vomiting and analyzing their bowel movements in a new Channel 5 reality show that promises to offer the ultimate form of exposure for struggling C-list stars.

THE INDEPENDENT (ENGLAND)

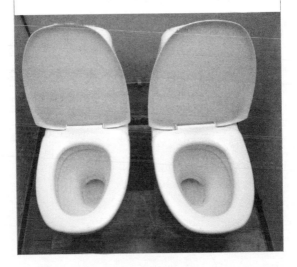

Taxes

Taxes. None of us like them, but most of us have to pay them. But we all wish we could pay *less*. Many of us cope with this by fudging a bit on our tax returns. Others try a more direct route.

> ## Can you lower my taxes, please? I was really unhappy with my tax bracket. I work hard and I want to keep my earnings.
>
> U.S. OPEN TENNIS CHAMPION VENUS WILLIAMS, IN A TELEPHONE CONVERSATION WITH PRESIDENT BILL CLINTON

Of course, the public doesn't think that changing definitions is enough. Some people have other ideas for tax innovation.

> *Like, a lot of us are making a lot of money now, and so we're paying a lot of taxes, you know. Is there, like, a way I can just write on the memo line of my check what I want my taxes to go for, like for school?*
>
> ACTRESS JUSTINE BATEMAN, AT A LECTURE GIVEN BY SENATOR JOHN KERRY (D-MASSACHUSSETTS)

But we think it's probably best to leave these things to the professionals. After all, the folks in the IRS are *highly* competent.

You will find it to be a distinct help ... if you know and look as if you know what you are doing.

IRS TRAINING MANUAL FOR TAX AUDITORS

Even so, the IRS seems almost naively optimistic about the honesty of taxpayers.

ILLEGAL INCOME, SUCH AS STOLEN OR EMBEZZLED MONEY, MUST BE INCLUDED IN YOUR GROSS INCOME.

HELPFUL INFORMATION POSTED ON THE OFFICIAL INTERNAL REVENUE SERVICE WEB SITE

It does its darnedest to make things simple and straightforward for us.

FOR PURPOSES OF PARAGRAPH (3), AN ORGANIZATION DESCRIBED IN PARAGRAPH (2) SHALL BE DEEMED TO INCLUDE AN ORGANIZATION DESCRIBED IN SECTION 501(C)(4), (5) OR (6) WHICH WOULD BE DESCRIBED IN PARAGRAPH (2) IF IT WERE AN ORGANIZATION DESCRIBED IN SECTION 501(C)(3).

INTERNAL REVENUE CODE

Passive activity income *does* not include the following: income for an activity that is not a passive activity.

IRS INSTRUCTIONS FOR FORM 8582, PASSIVE ACTIVITY LOSS LIMITATIONS

Maybe these kinds of instructions are why . . .

Hundreds of dogs have not paid their taxes

STORM LAKE (IOWA) *REGISTER*

Team Spirit

Sports is about the faith that you and your team will *win* . . . even against the odds. Coaches like Vince Lombardi were famous for these "never say die" attitudes. That spirit still exists today. Modern coaches *believe* in their teams.

It's not how good you can play when you play good. It's how good you play when you play bad, and we can play as bad as anyone in the country.

UNIVERSITY OF GEORGIA
BASKETBALL COACH HUGH DURHAM

This is because they feel so strongly about
their sport.

REPORTER: *Is there anything this team does well?*

BASKETBALL COACH: *Not really.*

REPORTER: *Are you making any progress?*

COACH: *I couldn't truthfully say that we are.*

REPORTER: *Do you like coaching the team?*

COACH: *I don't care that much for basketball.*

INTERVIEW WITH THE COACH OF THE FRIENDSVILLE ACADEMY (TENNESSEE) FOXES BASKETBALL TEAM, WHICH HAD CHALKED UP 138 CONSECUTIVE LOSSES

And they have a knack for "firing up"
their players for the next game.

HEY, THIS ISN'T OVER UNTIL THEY BEAT US TOMORROW.

TORONTO BLUE JAYS MANAGER CITO GASTON, BEFORE A LOSS TO THE TWINS

This "can do" attitude is transmitted to
their players.

I think we played hard, but it was a lackadaisical hard.

NEW JERSEY NETS GUARD OTIS BIRDSONG,
ON WHY THE TEAM HAD LOST AN NBA GAME

Not to mention the team's sportscasters.

A LOT OF GOOD BALL GAMES ON TOMORROW, BUT WE'RE GOING TO BE RIGHT HERE WITH THE CUBS AND THE METS.

CHICAGO CUBS BROADCASTER
THOM BRENNAMAN

Telephones

Telephones keep on getting more and more sophisticated—with more bells and whistles than ever before.

Perhaps this is why the manufacturers seem to think we, the consumers, need explicit instructions to understand the highly technical fine points of phone operation.

> **TO PLACE OR ANSWER A CALL, LIFT THE HANDSET. TO PLACE A CALL, DIAL THE DESIRED NUMBER. TO END THE CALL, HANG UP THE HANDSET. . . . TO PUT A CALL ON HOLD, PRESS "HOLD."**
> LUCENT TECHNOLOGIES TELEPHONE INSTRUCTION BOOK (MODEL 6210)

DO NOT PUT LIT CANDLES ON PHONE.

INSTRUCTIONS FOR A CORDLESS PHONE

How helpful! And phone companies are just as eager to offer their well-known brand of customer service to us.

Dear Mr. Cook:

We have attempted on several occasions to reach you by telephone to discuss payment of your telephone account—which was recently disconnected.

LETTER SENT FROM THE PHONE COMPANY

As for directories offered by local phone companies? Well, we *all* know how useful they are.

Federal Bureau of Investigation (718) 459-3140

If No Answer Call (718) 459-3140

NASSAU COUNTY NYNEX TELEPHONE DIRECTORY LISTING, 1991

Yes, it's no wonder everyone loves the phone company. It's so trustworthy!

You don't have to do anything to permit us to use your information. We think that's one reason you trust us.

QWEST BROCHURE EXPLAINING TO ITS CUSTOMERS THAT QWEST WILL START SHARING CUSTOMER INFORMATION WITH OTHER COMPANIES WITHIN 30 DAYS UNLESS THE CUSTOMER CALLS TO PROTEST (QWEST WAS NOT ANSWERING ITS PHONES.)

Television Listings

It's a good idea to scrutinize your television listings page closely. You never know what great shows you might be missing.

There are new twists on old favorites . . .

Movie: *Of Human Bandage.*

10:30 (8) *Shane* ('53) Alan Ladd, Jean Arthur. Former gunfighter, determined to establish peaceful life, must strap on his girl again in defense of homesteaders

And the shows you never ever imagined they'd put on prime time . . .

(TH.) BREAST FROM 20,000 FATHOMS: 1953/PAUL CHRISTIAN. PREHISTORIC BREAST MAKES IT WAY FROM ARCTIC DOWN TO NEW YORK CITY TO SCARE PEOPLE THERE. BEASTLY.

ORLANDO, FLORIDA, NEWSPAPER

. . . and very *unusual* holiday fare (some of which might not be suitable for the kids).

8:30: I Love Christmas. *A treat for nostalgia lovers. . . . Featuring clips from such film classics as* The Snowman *and* Chitty Chitty Gang Bang.

SUTTON COLDFIELD (ENGLAND) OBSERVER

At other times you get the feeling that whoever is writing the listing is editorializing a wee bit.

8:30 THE MOST EVIL MEN AND WOMEN IN HISTORY

QUENTIN WILSON REVEALS SOME OF THE MORE FANCIFUL EXCUSES GIVEN BY SPEEDING MOTORISTS TO AVOID PICKING UP POINTS ON THEIR LICENSES, WHILE TIFF NEEDELL TEST-DRIVES THE NEW MGTF.

LONDON *EVENING STANDARD*

(4) PRICE IS RIGHT: *TOPIC: PROSTITUTION AMERICAN STYLE*

STEWART, FLORIDA, NEWSPAPER

How to protect your neighborhood against crime and Jennifer Beals, star of *The Bride.* Live at Five.

NIGHTLY NEWS LINEUP FOR WCBS-TV, NEW YORK

GRAND SLAM: *CAROL VORDEMAN AND JAMES RICHARDSON ARE JOINED BY MORE TALENTED CONTESTANTS*

THE GUARDIAN (ENGLAND)

Still other times, you get the odd notion that whoever is writing the listing isn't a sports fan.

10:30 BOWLING: SUPERBOWL XXXV

THE SUNDAY TIMES OF SINGAPORE

Times, Tough

Extremely rich people have it easy. Or do they? Is everything a bowl of cherries for them? No. No, even the extremely rich have to deal with tough times.

I knew nothing of reality until Mummy died. She'd shielded us from everything. And then suddenly I was having to deal with the butler, the two chauffeurs, the cook, and everyone else.

SOCIALITE CHARLOTTE BROWN (NÉE DE ROTHSCHILD), IN *THE (LONDON) SUNDAY TIMES*

And they have to face difficult situations that don't arise for us hoi polloi—like the potential cancelation of Concorde flights.

Concorde is essential for the Duchess of York, who uses it to fly to America for her work with Weight Watchers. Without it she would be at a loss, as it would mean she cannot do the school run on Monday because she would have to leave on Sunday night. Because she is a mother and values time with her family, not being able to use the Concorde would seriously impact on her life. Things would definitely be a lot more stressful for her.

LONDON *EVENING STANDARD* (SADLY, IN SPITE OF THE DIFFICULTIES CAUSED FOR FERGIE, THE CONCORDE WAS INDEED CANCELED.)

It's even tougher for extremely rich celebrities. Unlike those who have merely inherited their fortunes (and their butlers, chauffeurs, et al.), they have to suffer for their multimillions.

Do you know what it's like to have to walk around in high heels and sing 35 songs a night, to have to diet to get into those dresses?

SINGER BARBRA STREISAND, EXPLAINING WHY SHE PLANNED TO RETIRE FROM TOURING

It's not as easy as it looks, being on all the time. I mean, what happens if I'm in a bad mood?

WHEEL OF FORTUNE COSTAR VANNA WHITE

But these rich celebrities know how to cope. Why, they're positively inspirational!

[The scene] was shot over two or three days when Matt [Damon] was aiming for his lowest weight. At the end of the second day he had a pizza standing by so he could eat. But we didn't finish the scene. It was so sad and he couldn't eat the whole thing until the next night. That's bravery.

ACTRESS GWYNETH PALTROW

Truth, Governmental

Politicians and government officials get a bad rap. Most people, for some odd reason, think they lie. All the time. About everything. We are happy to tell you that this is not the case. Sometimes politicians and government officials are honest. *Painfully* honest.

> **STATE SENATOR ERNEST A. JOHNSON, SEEKING REELECTION, SAID, "I HAVE MADE NO WILD PROMISES, EXCEPT ONE—HONEST GOVERNMENT."**
>
> *WORCESTER (MASSACHUSSETTS) SUNDAY TELEGRAM & GAZETTE*

Ask a politician a straight question and
you might actually get a straight answer!

> **REPORTER:** *What has been the most
> important legislation passed in this
> session?*
>
> **FLORIDA STATE SENATOR MALLORY HORNE:**
> *Well, passed . . . uh, you'd have to . . .
> uh, really, say that most of it at this
> juncture is, uh, still in the wings. Um,
> we have, uh, hold that a minute, I
> can't think of a darn thing we've
> passed.*

Maybe the trick is to catch them off guard.

> ## THIS IS THE MOST IMPORTANT BILL OF THE SESSION. . . . I HAVE NOT READ THE BILL.
>
> LOUISIANA STATE REP. SHERMAN COPELIN (D-NEW
> ORLEANS), DISCUSSING A BILL IN THE LOUISIANA
> LEGISLATURE

Or to listen in on a legislative debate.

I've had just about all of this good government stuff I can stand.

LOUISIANA STATE SENATOR CHARLES JONES (D-MONROE),
DURING A DEBATE IN THE LOUISIANA LEGISLATURE

Sometimes politicians are so frank, they might regret it later.

I've bought horses before. I've bought horse races before. I mean . . .

LOUISIANA STATE SENATOR KEN HOLLIS (R-METAIRIE), DISCUSSING A HORSE RACING BILL

In some cases, politicians put an unusual spin on "truth."

My problem was, I was too honest with you the first time.

REP. TILLIE FOWLER (R-FLORIDA) TO HER CONSTITUENTS,
EXPLAINING WHY SHE HAD CHANGED HER MIND ABOUT TERM LIMITS

But other times they come clean and lay it right on the line.

I'M A POLITICIAN, AND AS A POLITICIAN, I HAVE THE PREROGATIVE TO LIE WHENEVER I WANT.

CHARLES PEACOCK, EX-DIRECTOR OF MADISON GUARANTY, EXPLAINING AND JUSTIFYING HIS WRITING OF A CHECK TO PRESIDENT BILL CLINTON'S CAMPAIGN

There are a lot of things we do that are irrelevant, but that's what the Senate is for.

SENATOR ALAN SIMPSON (R-WYOMING), ON THE *MACNEIL/LEHRER NEWSHOUR*

THE BOTTOM LINE IS, THERE HAVE BEEN A LOT OF NUTS ELECTED TO THE UNITED STATES SENATE.

SENATOR CHARLES GRASSLEY (R-IOWA) ON WHY REPUBLICANS SHOULD SUPPORT OLIVER NORTH FOR HIS SENATE RUN IN 1994

See, there *are* some honest politicians out there. Lucky us! We think . . .

Utterances, Regrettable

The man or woman in the public eye invariably makes a slip or two when speaking. Don't we all? The problem is when the slip sounds a little racy . . . or racist. Take, for example, these not-so-great ways to win the black vote.

> **My heart is as black as yours!**
>
> NEW YORK CITY MAYORAL CANDIDATE MARIO PROCACCINO, MAKING SPEECH TO BLACK AUDIENCE

THAT'S ALL VERY WELL, BUT TWO BLACKS DON'T MAKE A WHITE.

BROADCASTER AND AUTHOR MICHAEL BARRATT, INTERVIEWING TWO ARGUING BLACK RHODESIAN POLITICIANS—AND MEANING TO SAY "TWO WRONGS DON'T MAKE A RIGHT."

And then there's this probably *former* spokesperson for Weight Watchers . . .

Some of our customers find it very daunting coming to a weight-loss advisory meeting. For some of them, it's difficult even to get through the door.

WEIGHT WATCHERS SPOKESPERSON DURING A RADIO INTERVIEW

But the best "let me rephrase that" moments come when sex intrudes with the foot in the mouth . . . no, let us rephrase that.

You must have had some famous players come through your hands over the years. [pause] I think I'll rephrase that.

TV SPORTSCASTER IN AN ON-AIR INTERVIEW

It used to be that you couldn't touch some girls with a ten-foot pole. Well, I was the guy with the twelve-foot pole.

TALK SHOW HOST MIKE DOUGLAS, DURING AN INTERVIEW WITH ACTRESS DYAN CANNON

Videos and DVDs

Watching videos and DVDs is now more than entertainment. It's *educational*.

How to Preserve Common Seaweeds

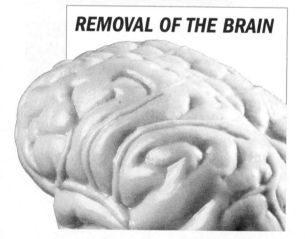

REMOVAL OF THE BRAIN

Sometimes we're not even sure exactly
what the film is about.

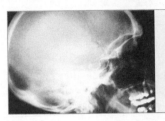

**Checking
for Head
Warpage**

Sometimes we are, but
we'd prefer not to think
about it too much.

**BEEF CATTLE
CASTRATION**

And still other videos answer questions
we've never
asked.

**How Pins Float
on Water**

Or they deal with things we thought
we pretty much knew already.

HOW A SCREW WORKS

Violence

Many of us are worried about violence in the media. Others, however, don't seem overwhelmingly concerned.

> **I don't think having a naked woman strapped to a rack is sexist at all. And I don't think the fact that we pretend to slit her throat is violent.**
>
> ROCK MUSICIAN BLACKIE LAWLESS OF W.A.S.P.

Media types like to point out that there's good violence and bad violence. Good violence is what *they* do.

> *Sure the body count in this movie bothers me, but what are you gonna do? It's what everybody likes. At least it's not an awful body count—it's a fun body count.*
>
> ACTRESS BONNIE BEDELIA, STAR OF *DIE HARD 2: DIE HARDER*

Some prominent media types agree that media violence inspires audiences to violence. But they don't always get the *whole* point.

I would say that anything that is indecent and violent in TV is a crime against humanity and they should shoot the head man responsible.

MEDIA MOGUL TED TURNER

Vomit

Vomit is not one of those things that crops up, so to speak, in most normal conversations. But some celebrities seem to have a thing for throwing up, usually as a way of expressing emotion. Then, of course, they share their vomiting moments with us, the eager public.

> **When I first read the script I gagged on it. Moments were so funny that I vomited from laughter.**
> DIRECTOR STEPHEN SPIELBERG, DESCRIBING HIS REACTION TO THE SCRIPT FOR HIS PEARL HARBOR BOMBING COMEDY (AND BOMB)

> **It was scary. I mean, sometimes I would be throwing up in my room just from the emotion, you know.**
> ACTOR PATRICK SWAYZE, ON PLAYING AN ANGRY CHARACTER IN CITY OF JOY

Sometimes celebrities can be really quite eloquent about the act of throwing up.

INTERVIEWER: *What has been your most memorable London meal?*

ACTRESS EMILY MORTIMER: *Mezzo with producer Stephen Evans. He suggested champagne to cure my hangover. He then asked if I could write a treatment for Lorna Sage's Bad Blood. Afterwards I vomited copiously outside Our Price. It was a prelapsarian moment, but now it seems quite portentous.*

IN A MAGAZINE INTERVIEW

Politicians tend to be more circumspect. They just talk about it as a possibility.

I would kind of like to throw up in living color.

REP. PAT SCHROEDER (D-COLORADO), REACTING TO CLINTON STRATEGIST DICK MORRIS'S SEX SCANDAL

The media tend to avoid the topic, but sometimes it "comes out" anyway.

It may have been officials throwing up in their hands in frustration, but the annual exodus to hometowns for the Idul Fitri celebration is a hard-earned right which cannot be denied.

JAKARTA (INDONESIA) POST

RICH ROLKERS IS THROWING UP IN THE BULLPEN.

SAN DIEGO PADRES SPORTSCASTER JERRY COLEMAN

In the best interest of the public, some forward-looking nations have "stepped in" to limit all this vomiting.

[Vomit] causes inconvenience when you are passing by and walking down the street.

REASON GIVEN BY OFFICIALS IN PHILIPPINE CITY WHO PASSED AN ORDINANCE AGAINST PUBLIC VOMITING, AS STATED IN THE *PHILIPPINE DAILY INQUIRER*

Other nations have valuable English trans-
lations for those unfortunate ones who
couldn't "hold it in."

I'm verry [sic] sorry
I clogged the sink. I
just didn't want to
vomit on the floor.

SENTENCE #12 IN THE JAPANESE BOOK *MAKING
EXCUSES IN ENGLISH*

And modern film—always on the cutting
edge—gets into the act, as well, with what is
probably the most unusual subtitle in history.

NO!

I SAW A VOMITING CRAB.

ENGLISH SUBTITLE OF A HONG KONG KUNG FU MOVIE

War, Thermonuclear

If the unthinkable happens and global thermonuclear war erupts, don't be too upset. Hard-working government experts have spent your tax dollars on studying the

NUCLEAR WAR COULD ALLEVIATE SOME OF THE FACTORS LEADING TO TODAY'S ECOLOGICAL DISTURBANCES THAT ARE DUE TO CURRENT HIGH-POPULATION CONCENTRATIONS AND HEAVY INDUSTRIAL POLLUTION.

U.S. OFFICE OF CIVIL DEFENSE OFFICIAL, 1982

potential impact of nuclear war and have come up with a lot of *positive*, uh, fallout.

It might be great for your wallet.

> [M]any taxpayers will be inconvenienced by the hostilities [of thermonuclear war] and will have to be excused from paying the normal rate of interest on their debts.
>
> IRS STUDY

Taxes might even go down!

> Consider a firm whose principal assets consist of a professional football team valued, preattack, at about $15 million. Suppose that the players survived the attack and that all debts of the team were fully paid up. Any plan to levy, for example, a net-worth tax postattack must face up to the fact that this firm's relative net worth in real terms is certainly not going to be the same as preattack.
>
> HENRY PESKIN, OFFICE OF EMERGENCY PLANNING OFFICIAL

And rest assured, the government will do all it can to make sure that utility check you wrote out will clear.

Following a nuclear attack on the United States . . . every effort will be made to clear trans-nuclear checks, including those drawn on destroyed banks. You will be encouraged to buy U.S. Savings Bonds.

FEDERAL EMERGENCY MANAGEMENT AGENCY, EXECUTIVE ORDER 11490, 1969

Of course, it won't all be gravy.

Nuclear war would certainly set back cable.
MEDIA MOGUL TED TURNER

Waste, Solid

Solid waste is more prevalent than you might think. Yes, poop pops up all over the place!

In baseball stadiums . . .

Jeff Bagwell appears to have this invisible stool underneath his rear end.

SPORTSCASTER TIM MCCARVER, REFERRING TO BAGWELL'S SQUATLIKE BATTING STANCE DURING THE 1999 ALL STAR GAME

Well, I see in the game in Minnesota that Terry Felton has relieved himself on the mound in the second inning.

KANSAS CITY ROYALS SPORTSCASTER FRED WHITE, READING A WIRE-SERVICE SUMMARY THAT MISTAKENLY SHOWED THE SAME STARTER AND RELIEF PITCHER FOR THE MINNESOTA TWINS

. . . and basketball arenas.

. . . and referee Richie Powers called the loose bowel foul on Johnson.

WASHINGTON SPORTS ANNOUNCER FRANK HERZOG DURING A BULLETS–TRAIL BLAZERS BASKETBALL GAME

On Wall Street . . .

The stock market took a big dump—er, ah, took a big drop, I should say.

NEWSMAN, KCRA-TV, SACRAMENTO, CALIFORNIA

. . . and in municipal parks.

THAT'S JUST ABOUT IT FROM KENO POOL. BACK TO YOU, VINCE AND CATHY. UH, DON'T MIND ME, I'M GOING TO TAKE A DUMP—DIP—RIGHT IN IT.

TV NEWSMAN, KPNX-TV, PHOENIX, ARIZONA, STANDING BESIDE A SWIMMING POOL

And, of course, there's political poop (and not quite the kind you're used to).

Everyone who is for abortion was at one time a feces.

BUSINESSMAN PETER GRACE, IN THE INTRODUCTION TO A RONALD REAGAN SPEECH

[SPENDING ON FEDERAL BENEFIT PROGRAMS IS GROWING] AT AN EXCREMENTAL RATE.

REPRESENTATIVE FRANK GUARINI (D-NEW JERSEY)

Some of the solid-waste coverage is a little . . . irregular.

The farmers in Annapolis Valley are pleased to announce that this year there will be an abundance of apples. This is particularly good news because most of the farmers haven't had a good crap in years.

MARYLAND TV NEWS BROADCASTER, DURING AN EARLY-MORNING REPORT

Perhaps those farmers could have learned something from the good citizens of Moorpark?

MOORPARK RESIDENTS ENJOY A COMMUNAL DUMP

NEWSPAPER HEADLINE

But let's dump—er, *drop*—this subject.

Wedding Announcements

Newspaper wedding announcements mark a hallowed milestone of life. Brides and grooms happily clip them for scrapbooks to show their grandchildren.

But sometimes the items contain a little too much in the way of what, er, literally happens in marriage . . .

> **Babe Treat wishes to announce the forthcoming marriage of her only daughter Patricia Elizabeth to William Andrew Bowman. The wedding is to be consummated on October 9, 1981 at Salmon Arm, B.C.**
>
> *THE WEEKENDER* (BRITISH COLUMBIA)

At other times, unwarranted and somewhat lurid visions of a very large, strong, and accommodating bride may pop up.

The bride, who was given away by her father, wore a dress of white figured brocade with a trailing veil held in place by a coronet of pearls. She carried a bouquet of rose buds and goods vehicles, leaving free access to all private vehicles not built for more than seven passengers.

ATHERSTONE (ENGLAND) NEWS AND HERALD

For some reason, heavy industrial imagery is also common.

THE BRIDE WORE A GOWN OF HEAVY OLDHAM CORPORATION GASWORKS.

MANCHESTER (ENGLAND) EVENING NEWS

Most announcements refer to the exchange of wedding vows. Some, however, mention exchanging quadrupeds.

Tonya Lynn Bruno and Mark Anthony Eagen will exchange wedding cows August 21 at St. Mary's Catholic Church

IDAHO NEWSPAPER WEDDINGS ANNOUNCEMENT PAGE

Sometimes, unfortunately, whoever wrote the wedding announcement just couldn't help editorializing . . .

The spacious home of Judge and Mrs. Woodbury was the scene of a beautiful wedding last evening when their youngest daughter, Dorothy, was joined in holy deadlock to Mr. Wilkie.

NEBRASKA NEWSPAPER

Mr. and Mrs. John Nash Wilding, of 880 Fifth Avenue, announce the engagement of their debatable daughter, Miss Virgin A. Wilding, to Mr. Luis Marcellinon de Avecedo of Buenos Aires.

NEW YORK TRIBUNE

Winning

What does it take to win? Let's ask our sports stars, managers, commentators, and fans for the *secrets of winning*.

He's pitched three or four games where, if we'd scored more runs for him, he would have won.

MILWAUKEE BREWERS MANAGER GEORGE BAMBERGER, AFTER A LOSS BY ONE OF HIS PITCHERS

Aha! That's the secret. Now let's hear from an average fan who makes it nice and succinct . . .

I THINK YOUR BEST CHANCE OF WINNING THE GAME IS TO BE AHEAD AT THE END.

MAN INTERVIEWED BY REPORTER ON TV

Or better yet, a star player . . .

YOU WOULDN'T HAVE WON IF WE HAD BEATEN YOU.
BASEBALL GREAT YOGI BERRA

And managers have their own insights.

The only reasons we're 7 to 0 is because we've won all seven of our games.
INTERIM CLEVELAND INDIANS MANAGER DAVE GARCIA

That about sums it up. So, now that we get the basic idea, let's go into specifics. First, how scoring fits into the big picture.

THEY HAVE WON 66 GAMES, AND THEY'VE SCORED IN ALL OF THEM.
SPORTSCASTER BRIAN MOORE

Sometimes winning gets a little tricky. Or should we say surrealistic?

I have a feeling that, if she had been playing against herself, she would have won that point.

SPORTSCASTER BOB HEWITT, COVERING A TENNIS MATCH

So you can win against yourself. You can also win against yourself in a tie. Yes, winning can be a little confusing.

TODAY PITTSBURGH BEAT THE PIRATES 6 TO 6!

SPORTSCASTER VINCE SCULLEY, DURING A DODGERS-ASTROS GAME, ANNOUNCING RESULTS OF A PITTSBURGH PIRATES-CHICAGO CUBS GAME

Sometimes it seems you can win without winning. Or something like that.

Andrea de Cesaris . . . the man who has won more Grands Prix than anyone else without actually winning one of them.

AUTO RACING COMMENTATOR MURRAY WALKER

Or win when you can't win.

I WAS IN A NO-WIN SITUATION, SO I'M GLAD THAT I WON RATHER THAN LOST.
BOXER FRANK BRUNO

But most of the time . . . well, let's hear from the manager of Oakland A's:

When you're not winning, it's tough to win a game.
OAKLAND A'S MANAGER TONY LA RUSS

Zero

Zero means nothing. Zip. Nada. Zilch. And, of course, nil (or so we'd always thought).

> **Tambay's hopes, which were nil before, are absolutely zero now.**
>
> AUTO RACING COMMENTATOR MURRAY WALKER

Yes, understanding the essence of zero is pretty basic stuff. But sometimes zero is apparently worth more than zero.

> ## ZERO-ZEROS ARE A BIG SCORE SOMETIMES.
> SPORTSCASTER RON ATKINSON

Still, most of us understand that zero is zero—no matter what spin is put on it.

During your time as a *Reader's Digest* customer, you have ordered at least 0 of our products. I do hope that the last product you ordered from us is still giving you pleasure.

FROM A READER'S DIGEST LETTER TO A CUSTOMER

Zoology, Game Show Contestants' Knowledge of

It's difficult to be an expert on the animal kingdom. After all, there are many different kinds of animals. No wonder game show contestants get confused when they're thrown a tough, technical mammal-related question.

HOST RICHARD DAWSON:
Name the most lovable breed of dog.

CONTESTANT: *Kitten.*

FAMILY FEUD

HOST RICHARD DAWSON:
Name a kind of bear.

CONTESTANT: *Papa Bear.*

FAMILY FEUD

Some are a little weak on insect-related questions too . . .

> **HOST ANNE ROBINSON:** *What insect is commonly found hovering above lakes?*
>
> **CONTESTANT:** *Crocodiles.*
>
> WEAKEST LINK

. . . while others have problems with primates. (Don't we all?)

> **HOST ANNE ROBINSON:** *Cro-Magnon was an early form of which mammal, which now numbers in the billions?*
>
> **CONTESTANT:** *Crabs.*
>
> WEAKEST LINK

But lack of knowledge doesn't stop these people! In many cases they just . . . well, wing it . . .

> **HOST ANNE ROBINSON:** *What does a bat use to facilitate flying in the dark?*
>
> **CONTESTANT:** *Wings.*
>
> WEAKEST LINK

⋮ . . . or rough it . . .

HOST LOUIS ANDERSON:
Name a word that a dog understands.

CONTESTANT: *Ruff.*

FAMILY FEUD

⋮ . . . or just go for broke.

HOST RICHARD KARN:
Name an animal whose eggs you probably never eat for breakfast.

CONTESTANT:
Hamster.

THE NEW FAMILY FEUD

ROSS and KATHRYN PETRAS, the brother and sister experts on all things stupid, are also the authors of *The 776 Stupidest Things Ever Said*, *The 776 Even Stupider Things Ever Said*, the bestselling *The 365 Stupidest Things Ever Said Page-A-Day® Calendar*, *Age Doesn't Matter Unless You're a Cheese*, *The Stupidest Things Ever Said by Politicians*, and *Unusually Stupid Americans*, among others. Ross Petras lives with his family in New Jersey; Kathryn Petras lives with her husband in Manhattan.